Testing Teachers

Testing Teachers
The Effect of School Inspections on Primary Teachers

Bob Jeffrey
and
Peter Woods

FALMER PRESS

Taylor & Francis Group

UK   Falmer Press, 1 Gunpowder Square, London, EC4A 3DE
USA   Falmer Press, Taylor & Francis Inc., 1900 Frost Road, Suite 101, Bristol, PA 19007

First published in 1998

A catalogue record for this book is available from the British Library

ISBN 0 7507 0787 9 cased
ISBN 0 7507 0786 0 paper

Library of Congress Cataloging-in-Publication Data are available on request

Jacket design by Caroline Archer

Typeset in 10/12pt Garamond by
Graphicraft Typesetters Limited, Hong Kong

Printed in Great Britain by Biddles Ltd., Guildford and King's Lynn on paper which has a specified pH value on final paper manufacture of not less than 7.5 and is therefore 'acid free'.

Contents

Acknowledgments

We are grateful to all the headteachers, deputy headteachers, teachers, pupils and other staff of all the schools involved for their time, openness, insights and cooperation in the research that has led to this book. In spite of being extremely busy at times and often wishing to put behind them some of the inspection events many teachers continued to support the research responding positively to the many visits by the researcher for up to a year or more after the experience. Some teachers found time to read some of the early drafts and their contributions were also gratefully received. Geoff Troman, Mari Louise Boyle and Denise Carlyle have all given valuable team support, stimulation and critique. We have benefited from being able to air some of these ideas at special Ofsted symposiums and for this we would like to thank Brian Fidler of Reading University and Vin Davis from Ofsted's Research department for their encouragement. Special thanks to Lisbeth for listening, reading, endlessly talking over issues and problems and for her insights and expertise; and to Kath for her unique brand of moral support. We have received valuable help from Aileen Cousins and many transcribers including Margaret Everett, Jan Giddings, Debbie Griffiths, Hilna Fontaine and Angela Burton.

This book is the result of research funded by the ESRC (R000236406) and The Centre for Sociology and Social Research at the School of Education, The Open University whom we thank for their support.

Chapter 4 has appeared in print previously as 'Feeling deprofessionalized: The social construction of emotions during an Ofsted inspection', *Cambridge Journal of Education*, **26**, 3, pp. 325–43, 1996. We thank the editors of this journal for permission to re-use the material here. An earlier version of Chapter 3 was presented at a European Educational Research Conference in Frankfurt 1997 and an earlier version of Chapter 5 was presented to the British Educational Research Association conference in York 1997.

Introduction

The Origins and Significance of OFSTED

The 1992 Education (Schools) Act inaugurated new national arrangements for inspection, overseen by the Office for Standards in Education (Ofsted). Ofsted has grown out of the 'New Right' ideology that gave rise to the educational reforms of the late 1980s and 1990s. The 'New Right' were not a homogeneous group, but most agreed with complaints of 'falling educational standards' (making comparison with economic competitors, especially West Germany); poor discipline within schools (both as a result of child-centred teaching methods, and of insufficient parental involvement in schools); 'producer capture' of education (Demaine, 1988, p. 252) — that is educationist dominance of school policies and programmes as compared to 'consumerist' i.e. parents and their children; and the influence of left-wing political values that promoted cooperation and equality and education for 'life' and for itself, and which demeaned competition, selection and instrumentalism. The 'New Right' was composed of two contrasting tendencies, 'cultural rightism' and 'classical liberal thought' (Jones, 1989). The latter was inspired by a spirit of consumerism, individual entrepreneurism, and competition — the values of the market — where the good drives out the bad; where what is good is decided by those immediately affected (the consumers) rather than by producers; where there are few controls so the 'good' is allowed to surface; and where people are motivated to do their best because they know it will be rewarded. The 'cultural rightists', on the other hand, emphasized 'the importance of a strong state to control the evils that an unregulated society is prey to' (ibid., p. 32).

The key to change was the principle of 'marketization' (giving more power to parents and governors), notably through 'open enrolment' and 'local management of schools'; and the apparently contradictory move towards centralization of power and control (this reflected the desire of the government argues Ball (1994), to gain the upper hand over local authorities, educationists and teachers, as opposed to the 'partnership' of the post-war years). The Government might claim that, for the moment at least, until the market became established, centralization was necessary to defeat these oppositional groups. The most prominent centralist measure was the establishment, without teacher consultation, of the National Curriculum and system of national assessment. These laid down what was to be taught and learned, and how it was to be assessed, in all state schools. Benchmarks for children's progress at certain ages, and common standards meant that schools, teachers and children could be compared, 'league tables' constituted, the successful rewarded (with more pupils, and hence more money, since parents, now free to choose, would send their children to these), and the 'failing' punished (with loss of pupils and eventually threat of closure).

Ofsted was set up to oversee this process, and to reinforce the drive for improved standards (see Wilcox and Gray, 1996, for an extended account of the origins of Ofsted). Its arrival signalled a new era for teachers. Research suggests that, hitherto, teachers have played more of an active interpretative role in implementation of government policy than is sometimes thought, given the heavily prescribed nature of it in recent years. After all, new policies have to be mediated through teachers (Penney and Evans, 1991; Ball and Bowe, 1992; Power, 1994; Vulliamy and Webb, 1993; Fitz, Halpin and Power, 1994). Our own previous work has drawn attention to the creativity and self-determination of primary teachers, and their capacity for appropriating the changes (Woods, 1995; Woods and Jeffrey, 1996b). Osborn and Broadfoot (1992) also noted that most of the teachers in their study appeared to be 'incorporating', that is 'a feeling that they will accept the changes, but will not allow anything considered really important to be lost' (p. 148; see also Pollard et al., 1994). Osborn and Broadfoot recognize that these may be only interim responses. The advent of Ofsted threatens to change this situation radically.

Ostensibly an independent body whose mission was to improve schools and teaching in the interests of raising educational standards (Ofsted, 1995), Ofsted nonetheless operates within the boundaries of the policy reforms outlined above. Arguably, its establishment represents a drive by central government for more control over the implementation process. Ofsted inspections are meant to have a direct effect on the policy and practices of schools. The fact that Ofsted inspections are a mass project across all state schools, and were notionally intended to take place every four years (now six), creates a climate within the education system in which the very concept of inspections becomes part of the 'education culture'. The idea of inspection in some shape or form has become part of the daily lives of schools.

Inspection Arrangements

The 1992 Schools Act set out the ground rules and empowered Her Majesty's Chief Inspector to set things up. The Office for Standards in Education (Ofsted), headed by Her Majesty's Chief Inspector (HMCI), is the independent, non ministerial government department with the task of devising a Framework for inspection which establishes the criteria for the conduct of inspections and of writing a Handbook for the inspection which gives detailed guidance to the independent inspectors. Ofsted also recruits, trains and assesses the inspectors, schedules the schools for inspection, awards inspection contracts to compet-ing teams, monitors the inspectors' performance and pays for the inspection.

Inspection teams vary in size from three to fifteen depending on the size of the school. They are led by a Registered Inspector (RgI) and include one lay member whose responsibilities will be prescribed by the RgI but is statutorily required to play a full part. The definition of layness describes someone who is not professionally engaged in teaching or educational administration. The majority of the inspectors in the system will probably have had experience with local authorities or as former HMIs (Her Majesty's Inspectors). Others will probably have come from teaching, further and higher education or from an educational administration background. All of them must satisfactorily complete an Ofsted training programme. The team is assembled by the RgI who tenders to Ofsted for inspections. Contracts are awarded strictly on the basis of 'value for money — that is an assessment of the quality of the team and its suitability to the school in question combined with the price quoted' (CSSS, 1994, p. 3). Schools neither pay for the inspections nor choose the teams but they can challenge members on the ground of a connection. A fortnight is allowed for the inspection process. A designated number of inspector days are made for each school depending on size and type of institution and these are used as observation days in the school, usually lasting no more than a week.

Prior to the inspection the RgI requests documentation from the school concerning its policies and characteristics. After the inspection a written report is prepared within six weeks and presented to the governors who have a further six weeks to prepare an action plan in response to the inspection team's recommendations. In the meantime, a summary is printed and used by the school to pass on information to parents. This plan is submitted both to Ofsted and the next annual parents' meeting. The RgI informs HMCI if he or she believes that the school is failing or is likely to fail to give its pupils an acceptable standard of education. If HMCI agrees with the RgI's evaluation then special measures designed to tackle the schools problems will apply.

In the school, the Ofsted handbook is used by the management to gain insight as to how to succeed. Invitations are issued to either Local Education Authority (LEA) teams of inspectors or private inspection contractors to carry out preliminary, trial inspections. In some cases the LEA delegates arrive uninvited to 'assist' with the preparation. This is an opportunity to get things into order (Sandbrook, 1996; Wilcox and Gray, 1996) and a chance to review working practices and policies. This preparation period is dominated by attempts by teachers to provide a series of policies that determine the school's work, and to show how the actual classroom work reflects those policies. Teachers are also concerned with the preparation of an image of their school and classrooms that they feel will be acceptable to the inspectors. This image concerns the visual displays, the cleanliness and good working order of the school, good classroom order, organisation and acceptable pedagogic approaches. The staff collectively develops a corporate climate where the success, or survival of the school becomes the dominant theme and all other interests, conflicts, and differentiated work become subsumed under the objective of satisfying the Ofsted inspectors.

The effects live on long after the inspection itself, such that the inspectors have been regarded as an 'absent presence' (Troman, 1997a) in the school. Consequently the process is much longer and more complex than it might appear. An examination of the whole process in depth is required which would include anticipatory and follow-up stages as well as the inspection itself, to understand its full import and in order to find answers to questions such as:

- What kind of educational, social and political event is an Ofsted Inspection?
- How are we to conceptualize it as a process?
- What effects does it have on teachers and on their work?
- How does it affect the traditional latitude in the policy implementation process?
- What are the implications for educational improvement?

Researching Ofsted Inspections and Their Effects

It was in this context that we began our research in 1995. We wanted to understand the process and structure of these inspections over all their phases; how they were conducted, what their functions were, and what the effects were, especially on teachers' work, and on their role, and identity. We also aimed to identify the strategies used by teachers in coping with the inspections, and to consider their relationship with their work. These seem to us crucial issues in any consideration of 'raising educational standards'.

In seeking answers to these, we conducted research in six contrasting primary schools in and around a large conurbation that had all undergone inspections during the period 1995–97. We engaged in detailed, qualitative research in each of the schools from the point of notification of an inspection (up to a year in advance), through the inspection itself, to a month afterwards, with occasional visits being made for several months beyond that. The field-worker (Bob) 'lived' the inspection with the teachers (Rose, 1990), conversing with them, observing them, studying documentation. Many of the discussions were tape recorded and transcribed. Using these techniques, we documented school changes in policy and teacher changes in classroom practice and planning. We monitored the process of being inspected, and studied the climate surrounding an inspection process. We recorded first hand reports of teachers' experiences at the time of the inspection. We observed teacher preparations for classroom visits by inspectors and recorded reactions immediately following. We also monitored the aftermath, and in particular, the effects of the inspection on school atmosphere and ethos, together with the effects of the process on the teachers' perceptions of self, role and career. We also consulted with the Registered Inspectors at each of the six schools in order to explore their perspectives on the exercise.

The schools were as follows (All names used for schools and teachers are pseudonyms):

Flately

Flately primary school was based in a three decker Victorian building and a low level 1980s modern building and served a large inner city estate built in the 1970s. At the time of the inspection it had a growing three form intake from predominately ethnic minorities. There were a considerable range of minority groups represented, with children of Nigerian origin and Vietnamese origin being the two largest groups alongside British Afro Caribbean and white children. Approximately one-third of the roll were identified as children with 'Special Educational Needs', though most were at the lowest level of need. There were two nursery classes taking two intakes daily. The school had specialist rooms for teaching and for resources. There was a cage for football in the playground and the whole perimeter was marked by a 20-foot high fence and surrounded by mid rise blocks of flats and a small garden area to which the children had restricted use. There were the equivalent of 25 staff of whom 4 were men.

Mixstead

This was a new, 3-year-old, two-decker open plan school with extensive grounds bounded by a quiet railway line, a distant main road and a large, open, private sports ground. It had its own area of woodland, various sports pitches and a separate car park. It was also bounded by a mixture of new semi-detached and terraced housing for re-housed people from the inner city but it also attracted wealthier parents who lived in the older part of the area. It had a station, a few shops nearby but few other amenities. It had a large nursery with two daily intakes and extensive grounds. The classrooms were all open plan and it was possible to watch much that went on below from the upper floor. A significant number of children came from one parent families. The deputy head did not have a class but floated between classes taking small groups. The Senior Management Team (SMT) consisted of five. There was a staff of 16 of whom 3 were men.

Morghouse

This was housed in a three decker late Victorian building taking up about 75 per cent of the available space. It was situated on the borders of the large city in an area dominated by owner occupied double fronted terraced and semi-detached 1930s housing. The intake was mainly professional and had a lower than average eligibility for free meals within the borough. There was one nursery class taking two intakes daily. The playground was large and generally barren. They made extensive use of the three halls for many school clubs. There were the equivalent of 12.6 teachers of whom 2 were men.

Lowstate

Lowstate was in the centre of a large low level housing estate on the edge of the large conurbation. Most of the terraced and many of the fewer semi detached houses are, or were once, council owned. It was mainly a white working class area. The school was situated around the corner from a well used parade of mainly service orientated shops. It was a low level school built in the 1940/50s with the infants on one level and the juniors on two floors. Some of the classrooms were quite large and the ground floor ones had doors leading out on to the playground. They had had some extensive building works in the previous year with every classroom being renovated. There was one nursery class taking two intakes. There were 13 staff, including 2 men.

Cottingly

Cottingly was a one level new school completed in 1991 with a history of serving a village on the outskirts of the city going back to 1873. At the time of the research the intake was a mix of white working class and children from more professional homes with a very small number of ethnic minority and special needs children. The building had classrooms with activity areas in the corridors and little storage space. The classrooms were all the same size and looked crowded with 30 plus pupils in them. They had a large grassed outside area, a large pond and woods available for use. Their budget was decreasing in real terms, according to the headteacher, who was very concerned about how she was going to maintain the same level of resources in the following year. They had the equivalent of 7.2 teachers, only one of whom was a man. They ran an extensive network of school clubs.

Trafflon

This was another three-decker Victorian school though smaller than Flately. The school buildings could accommodate twice their roll at the time of the research so there were some large classrooms and many resource areas available. It was located less than a mile from the centre of the city and was close to congested traffic. It served mainly 1960s high rise estates and some low level accommodation. The area was run down with many services closed and derelict. Its intake was mainly of Caribbean origin, white working-class and a small number of pupils from the Asian continent. Nearly half their children were identified as requiring Special Educational Needs though most of these are at the lowest level of need. They had a teaching staff equivalent to 6.5 women and 1 male

Table 1.1:   *Summary of school sample*

School	Role	Full Time Equivalent Staffing including the head	P/T Ratio	Eligibility for Free Dinners	English as a Second Language
Flately	578	25.00	23.12 : 1	73%	66%
Mixstead	410	16.80	24.40 : 1	18%	13%
Morghouse	316	12.60	25.00 : 1	16%	1%
Lowstate	295	13.00	22.70 : 1	48%	9%
Cottingly	206	8.20	25.10 : 1	14%	1%
Trafflon	165	7.50	22.00 : 1	47%	48%

nursery teacher. Two of the teachers had been at the school for over twenty years and they also had one volunteer ex-teacher who worked in the school three days a week. A significant amount of play space was available for such a small roll.

A summary of the main school details is given in Table 1.1. A summary of the basic details of teachers in the six schools follows in Table 1.2.

Teacher Summary

There were 79 teachers in the 6 schools of whom 85 per cent were women. Of the 6 headteachers, 3 were men. There were 7 deputy heads (Flately had 2 deputies), 2 of whom were men.

In the text of the book, only the name and the school of the teacher concerned is given unless other information is directly relevant. Further information can be gained from the tables below. In analysing the data, we have considered what it is that all six inspections have in common and how they differ. We have noted similarities and differences within schools and among teachers across schools and we have looked for common properties in these formations, and the conditions that attend them. We make no claim that these reactions are generally representative of all schools and all inspections — though we do feel, from reports in the press, from the work of Ofstin (1997), other research (Brimblecombe et al., 1995; Sandbrook, 1996; Wilcox and Gray, 1996; Fitz-Gibbon, 1996), and reactions to conference presentations we have made at BERA (British Educational Research Association) that they are not at all unusual, and that they demand attention. The explanations we advance for the conflicts and contradictions we discovered do have a more general relevance. They are available to others to apply to their situations, to test, and if necessary modify or elaborate.

Structure and Orientation of the Book

We begin with episode 1 of the story of the inspection week of one of our schools as recorded by Bob Jeffrey in field notes and we continue the story by

Table 1.2: Teacher Details

School Name Pseudonym	Gender/Age/ Approximate Years Teaching	Teaching Group KS1/2–Key Stage One/Two EY–Early Years P/T–Part Time Float	Status and Responsibilities HT–Headteacher DH–Deputy HD–Head of Dept. PH–Postholder	Life Circumstances P–Partner D–Dependent S–Single
Flately				
Gayle	F/30–40/15	KS1		S
George	M/20–30/2	KS1		P
Georgina	F/30–40/12	KS1	PH	PD
Glen	M/20–30/4	KS2	PH	PD
Gloria	F/30–40/15	KS1		PD
Grace	F/40–50/24	KS2	DH	P
Gwen	F/30–40/10	EY		PD
Leila	F/30–40/8	KS2	PH	P
Raymond	M/50–60/14		HT	P
Rebecca	F/30–40/8	KS2	PH	PD
Rob	M/40–50	KS2	SMT	PD
Robina	F/30–40/10	EY	HD	P
Rosa	F/30–40/12	KS2		S
Ruth	F/40–50	Float	Technician	P
Sandra	F/20–30/2	KS1		P
Shereena	F30–40/16	Float	PH	P
Sherina	F/30–40/3	KS2		PD
Shona	F/30–40/12	KS2	PH	P
Shula	F/30–40/10	KS1	DH	PD
Smica	F/20–30/1	KS1		P
Sophie	F/30–40/15	KS2	PH	SD
Susanna	F/50–60/28	KS1		P
Tony	M/20–30/2	KS2	Supply Teacher	S
Cottingly				
Becky	F/40–50/25	KS1	PH	SD
Bronwyn	F/40–50	KS2	PH	PD
Francis	F/40–50/5	KS2	PH	PD
Frank	M/60+/30	KS2	DH	S
Freda	F/20–30/4	KS2		P
Frederica	F/50–60/24	KS1	PH	P
Hannah	F/40–50/8	NONE	HT	PD
Helen	F/20–30/2	KS1		P
Trafflon				
Carl	M/50–60/20	Float	Volunteer	P
Carol	F/40–50/23	KS1	PH	S
Clare	M/40–50/22	Float	Part Time	PD
Cloe	F/40–50/23	KS2	PH	SD
Colin	M/30–40/10	EY	HD	PD
Corrine	F/30–40/4	KS2		SD
Tania,	F/50–60/25	KS1	PH	P
Toni	F/30–40/13	KS1	DH	S
Veronica,	F/40–50/12	KS2	PH	S
Victor	M/40–50/6	None	HT	PD
Morghouse				
Dan	M/40–50/8	Cover	HT	PD
Deena	F/30–40/15	KS1	SMT	PD
Diane	F/40–50/17	KS2	PH	PD
Dora	F/50–60/24	KS1	SMT	S
Nancy	F/30–40/15	KS1	PH	PD
Naomi	F/30–40/15	KS2	PH	SD

Table 1.2: (cont'd)

School Name Pseudonym	Gender/Age/ Approximate Years Teaching	Teaching Group KS1/2–Key Stage One/Two EY–Early Years P/T–Part Time Float	Status and Responsibilities HT–Headteacher DH–Deputy HD–Head of Dept. PH–Postholder	Life Circumstances P–Partner D–Dependent S–Single
Nathan	F/20–30/8	KS2	PH	P
Nell	F/30–40/15	KS1		PD
Nesta	F/40–50/22	KS1		SD
Neville	M/30–40/10	KS2	PH	P
Norman	M/30–40/18	KS2	DH	PD
Lowstate				
Aileen	F/40–50/22	KS1		PD
Amy	F/30–40/6	KS2		SD
Angelina	F/40–50/20	Float	DH	PD
Ava	F/40–50/20	EY	HD	P
Edith	F/20–30/1	KS1		P
Elvira	F/30–40/10	EY	Nursery Nurse	DP
Esther	F/40–50/22	KS2	PH	PD
Evelyn	F/30–40/10	KS2	SMT	P
Larry	M/30–40/15	KS2	SMT	PD
Laura	F/30–40/17	KS2	PH	S
Leila	F/30–40	Float	Part Time	PD
Letica	F/30–40/15	KS1		SD
Linda	F/30–40/6	KS2		SD
Lional	M/40–50/20	KS2	SMT	PD
Lois	F/50–60/15		HT	P
Lola	F/30–40/15	EY		PD
Tracy	F/30–40/4	KS1		SD
Mixstead				
Enid	F/50–60/25	KS2	SMT	PD
Erica	F/20–30/1	KS2		P
Evelyn	F/40–50/10	KS1	Supply	
Katherine	F/20–30/1	KS2		P
Katrina	F/50–60/22	KS1	PH	PD
Kay	F/30–40/12	KS1		PD
Kayleigh	F/40–50/20	KS1	Part Time	PD
Keith	M/20–30/2	KS2		S
Kieran	M/40–50/22	KS2	SMT	PD
Kirsty	F/40–50/20	KS1	Part Time	PD
Otterley	F/40–50/22	EY	HD	PD
Rachael	F/50–60/15		HT	SD
Reen	F/50–60/30	KS2	SMT	P
Rita	F/30–40/17	Float	Γ	P
Roger	M/30–40/10	KS2		S
Rosa	F/30–40/15	Float	Part Time/PH	PD
Rose	F/30–40/8	KS2	PH	PD

inserting further episodes in between the main chapters of the book. It is a typical story, at least as far as our six schools are concerned. It relates some of the events of the week from the Friday, before the Monday when the inspection itself began, to the Friday evening when the teachers celebrated the end of the inspection. It is a story constructed at the time as seen through the eyes of the researcher. No attempt is made to analyse or to invoke theory. Rather, the aim is to try to recreate the atmosphere of the event, to portray the feel and mood of it, and to convey the reader into the heart of one of the schools, as a prelude to the analysis that follows. The methodology involved is discussed at length in Woods and Jeffrey (in Woods, 1996). Readers are referred especially to Chapter 6, 'Living and Researching a School Inspection'.

Analysis follows in the remaining five chapters. In Chapter 1 the RgIs' perspectives are viewed through their account of their values, their experience of the inspection process, their position in relation to Ofsted, their supervisory role as lead inspectors and their view concerning their relationships with the teachers and schools. The Ofsted Framework through which they work uses a managerialist discourse but the inspectors feel that they mediate it with a more humanistic approach. We argue that this is how the inspectors resolve the basic contradiction between the technicism of the Ofsted model and their own personal values. In the main, they see inspection as a necessary event to improve schools and to develop equality of opportunity for all pupils. They generally feel that the distance achieved by their role in the event is a productive one in terms of objective judgment and that this is seen as valuable by the schools. They accept that accountability is a necessary method of operationalizing policy, and point out that they are themselves accountable. They are, in effect, 'positioned' between the institution of Ofsted and the schools and in coping with this they accept a certain amount of isolation. However, whatever humanistic elements inspectors felt they were importing into their methods, few of them were picked out in the teachers' reactions. This suggests that the inspectors were operating in two contrasting contexts, an idealistic context in which they constructed their own meanings of inspections influenced by personal beliefs and values, and an implementational context where managerialism prevailed (Keddie, 1971).

Chapter 2 exemplifies the nature of this conflict. The language of the Ofsted Framework on which inspectors base their work is a technical one steeped in the concepts of functionality and the use of the measurement of components to evaluate a school's effectiveness. These primary teachers, on the other hand, valued qualitative engagements, holistic development and multivariable measurements of the pupil as person. They valued human relationships, sensitivity, a constructivist approach to learning rather than distanced evaluation, numerical assessments and a 'testing' culture. This conflict is explored in four key areas of their work, knowledge, pedagogy, assessment and culture. They questioned the validity of the inspection process, the promotion of disputed pedagogic approaches and curriculum organization, the quality of the assessment procedures and a shift in school culture from professional to technical relations. Most teachers did not object to inspection as a concept for they fully acknowledged their accountability to both the community and the government, but the foci and form of the inspection was generally felt to be inappropriate.

In Chapter 3 we analyse how inspectors' power represents an example of what Foucault (1977) calls 'disciplinary power' which seeks to produce well ordered organizations, and efficient, productive and disciplined people. The effect of this downward surge of power is a colonization of teachers' time and space which includes their non teaching lives, their physical well being, their beliefs and individuality. Hours at work increase as do hours spent at home on inspection demands. The teachers, mainly women, struggle with increased demands on their time and family members are brought into the Ofsted process to assist them. The Ofsted process, for a year or more prior to the event, gradually becomes the central focus for most of the teachers. The school experience is supplemented by a 'discourse of derision' (Ball, 1990b) from politicians and the media, with the latter producing, almost daily, reminders for teachers that inspection is not far away.

In Chapter 4 we take the case of one of our schools to illustrate a common effect among all of them. We argue that the technicist approach of the inspectors impacted against the holistic and humanistic values of the teachers, producing a high degree of trauma among the teachers. This trauma was not a simple emotional response of the moment, nor was it a product of school failure or lack of leadership, since neither of these applied. It was, rather, socially and politically constructed. The teachers' reactions have to be seen against the background of the government's managerialist reforms. In this context, the particular emotions released suggest that the inspection analysed here had a latent function of deprofessionalization. Professional uncertainty was induced, with teachers experiencing confusion, anxiety, professional inadequacy and the marginalization of positive emotions. They also suffered an assault on their professional selves, closely associated among primary teachers with their professional roles (Nias, 1989) and the inspection caused 'negative trauma' rather than 'positive trauma' (D. Hargreaves, 1983). One of the ways for teachers to avoid such negative trauma is by shifting identity and status from the professional to a technical role.

Some may indeed do this, but a number of our teachers employed a range of coping strategies in order to maintain their values and beliefs, their professional identities, and their equilibrium, as we discuss in Chapter 5. Some teachers managed this process more equably than others with some enhancing themselves, others complying with varying degrees of willingness, some reconstructing themselves, and with some not coping at all (Woods et al., 1997). On the whole, teachers showed considerable skill, creativity and flexibility in developing their own professional discourse (Woods and Jeffrey, 1996a), employing humour, distancing themselves from Ofsted itself, asserting themselves, developing solidarity, and, at the same time, immersing themselves in the event itself. They adjusted to varying demands, at times being defensive, at others appropriating the process, confronting it. They distanced themselves to maintain identity and engaged with the process to play the game and to maintain corporateness. At the same time they positioned themselves in relation to the inspectors to maintain or enhance the self and their professionality. The study as a whole shows the effects of the whole general broad drift toward managerialism and technicization enacted in government policy in recent years.

The general culture of inspection that teachers now live in acts as a constraint independently of any particular inspection, such that teachers' 'positioning' formulates long in advance of the inspection week itself in response to the general trend. Compared to this influence, the inspectors' humanistic touches appear cosmetic. The general managerialist trend continues, with inspectors and teachers coping as best they can, making little real contact across the structural divide.

Notes from the Field (1)
Inspection Week at Lowstate

Weekend Calm

The place is Lowstate school. It's 10.10 on Saturday morning. I've been allowed into the school to research the effects of Ofsted inspections on primary teachers. I'm sitting in the infant hall with my back to the windows facing the display boards. It is very quiet and a contrast to the normal buzz and chatter of a school. I can hear a blackbird singing in the garden. The light, albeit filtered through tall pot plants climbing up the large window frames, shows up the highly polished floor. Every display board has a uniform three centimetre border made from black sugar paper — one was removed because it didn't conform. The contents of the displays are all mounted and uniform computer printed labels explain the contents or challenge the reader to respond mutely. There are few teacher written labels.

The lower school corridor has all its display boards backed with hessian and on them are mounted photographs of pupils and school events together with prints of classic pictures. One display records the achievements of women in history and a large window is covered with a display depicting a Victorian street. The PE and dining hall are devoid of displays except for functional notices relating to PE equipment. One of the two staircases to the upper school have framed glass fronted pictures on the walls, (the last of these put up on the Sunday morning by the Premises Officer). The other staircase, rarely used and known as 'the back staircase', has a photographic display of some site building works with artefacts such as bricks and pipes displayed on the window sill. The headteacher and husband mounted these on a previous weekend. The main hall in the upper school is totally covered with a school journey display that spills out onto the corridor. Every piece of wall is covered with over four hundred treble mounted pieces of work and photographs representing this year's journey to Kent. The window sills are used to display artefacts and folders of children's work.

The hall is set up for assembly on Monday. There is a newish lectern bought by the head after she first heard about the Ofsted visit and in keeping with the school's developing emphasis on religious assemblies. (She hoped that the lectern would bring 'a sense of awe'. Some teachers would have preferred the money spent on books.) There are two matching chairs on either side of the lectern and two tall pot plants further back flanking the lectern and the chairs. A music stand is set to one side waiting for a child to play some music. Large printed numbers have appeared on the walls in recent days to indicate where each class should sit. I thought at first they were hymn numbers. As I slide quietly along the corridors poking my head in the classrooms I'm struck by how the teachers' desks have magically grown spaces and how items are neatly placed upon them. A large plastic bag is spread over one desk as if to remind the teacher to finally fill it with any extraneous and unwanted material.

As I contemplate the school's quiet confidence it is punctuated from time to time with sounds from a classroom, the moving of furniture, the playing of some music, the hammering of a staple gun, the sudden whistling of a teacher briskly leaping down the stairs or more unusually the burst of laughter from two or three teachers gathered in a corridor or a particular room. The silence is again disturbed by the low hum of two petrol lawn mowers as they circle the lone willow tree cutting the grass of the main green play area. This is Saturday morning and one wonders if the workers are getting overtime. The Premises Officer is playing his full part in the preparation. The staff have already commented on the surprise of having new locks on the loo doors.

The school is at peace for a while, proud of its self and awaiting the inspection event with a quiet self assurance. It is a calmness which has grown from exacting preparation and a feeling of inevitability that they can't do any more and they have done their best.

As I leave, early in the afternoon, I hear some teachers making arrangements to meet in the nearest shopping centre for coffee and a late lunch. They seem to have it under control. All is nearly ready for the inspection event.

It's 10.10 again on Sunday morning. As I enter the upper school building I can hear the drip of water in the toilet cisterns. There is a strong gale force wind and the beautiful Montana clematis is being blown vigorously on a playground trellis. This contrasts with the calmness inside the school. I can hear quiet voices in the smoking room.

One classroom is a mess and contrasts dramatically with the rest of the school. It is a large, unused, newly decorated classroom full of musical instruments. Different sized folders and children's trays full of work have been dumped on the floor, the piano top, on shelves, unit tops and tables. Some of the trays have soft red folders in them, pupil's school folders with records and work samples from their entry into school. Some are full to the brim with topic folders, books and models such as kites, windmills, fans, constructed vehicles and coloured spinners. There is great variety in both the abundance and quality of material presented, reflecting possibly the differences in teaching styles and of the teachers as people. The trays are offerings to the inspection team, evidence of three levels of children's work — above average, average and below average.

The headteacher and the deputy headteacher sit next to one another in the latter's room writing quietly. Aileen talks to herself in the music room as she still shuffles through the trays. Larry is on his knees cutting up paper and mounting pictures with paper strewn all over the floor. His wife drifts in and out assisting him. Amy cuts up more labels and attempts to make them uniform. Lional writes up some sums on a large piece of paper and his wife mounts fabric pictures and we three listen to the last 10 minutes of a dramatic episode of the Archers. The Premises Officer is seen fixing doors, putting up the last of the cased pictures on the staircase. Aileen sits on her carpet sewing up large cushion covers.

All is nearly ready for the inspection event.

At last Aileen says, 'I can leave that. I can finish it in the morning before school' and she packs up to go home for a late lunch. In Evelyn's room Monday's date is on the blackboard and the chairs are neatly set out. Her desk is immaculate with four piles of papers placed neatly next to each other. The reading books look as though they have all been placed on the shelves in a neat order. In Linda's room there is not a book or a piece of paper out of place, the chairs are neatly set at the tables and her desk is very tidy and ordered. In the nursery the Monday morning activities — painting, cooking, modelling — are laid out on the tables, the house is on the carpet and the three descending sized bears sit at a breakfast table in the home corner as in the Goldilocks story. In Tracy's room all is set and the ticking of the clock reminds me that it's only now a matter of hours before the actual event. I hear the wind cause the builder's gates to crash together. The weather is stormy but a calmness permeates the school. Leila, a part time teacher, drops in a tin of biscuits for the staff. She has been thinking about them most of the night.

All is now ready for the inspection.

The Prologue

On Monday at 8.15 the car park is full to overflowing. 'It looked like a motor-way service station.' All the inspectors drive cars no more than 18 months old. A Mazda Xedes 6, an Audi A4, a Honda Elite Civic, an Escort and a Fiat Tipo, believed to belong to the lay inspector, stand bright and gleaming amongst the teachers' older cars.

I have restricted myself to the staff room during the day and as I make my way there I don't meet anyone. The teachers are already in their classrooms. The staff room is deserted, only the occasional sound of the water heater is heard. Ava, the job share nursery teacher is the first to come into the staff room, She has come in to see what the inspectors look like and to wish the staff good luck for she doesn't officially begin work until later in the week. She comments on new displays she has seen around the school. 'It's like a living exhibition. Lots of new resources had been bought recently and kept for Ofsted like the RE books that I only handed out this week'. She is nostalgic for the old, local inspection where you had a chance to explain things, 'they knew you as friends'. She describes how the Chair of Governors appeared in the school at 8.10 and visited every classroom to wish all the teachers good luck. 'It was like inspecting the troops before the battle, like Monty did, to show how the general cared about them.'

At 8.38 Amy, Laura and Linda enter with the latter yawning. Angelina enters soon afterwards and says she has butterflies but they're good to get the adrenaline going. She is followed by Evelyn who declares in a slightly jocular manner that 'her husband is lost at sea'. He was skippering a sailing boat with secondary school pupils and because of the gales yesterday had to shelter in France until this morning. She described her run on Sunday — 6 miles in 58 minutes — and said she had watched the lottery results on Saturday night for the first time. The atmosphere is a more spirited one compared with the calm of Saturday and Sunday.

At 8.44 the rest of the staff appear. There is much talk and occasional jocularity, 'I couldn't find any clean clothes this morning'. There are three boxes of sweet things, milk chocolate marshmallows, a packet of dark and white chocolate biscuits and a tin of butterscotch shortbread on the main central table around which people sit. The marshmallows are opened and Angelina and Aileen declare they are 'eating for Ofsted'. Most of the teachers have put on their smarter clothes.

At 8.47 the inspection team led by the Registered Inspector enter the room. There are three women and one man. They too are smartly dressed with jackets and the man has a bronzed tan. The RgI smiles and states that this is the worst bit for the teachers but it will whizz past and she laughs. She says they will be exhausted by Wednesday and not to worry for it is known as 'dip day' — where enthusiasm drains away and tiredness is felt most strongly — and there is general laughter. (In the event the teachers described it 'not as dip day but kick day' and a 'self fulfilling prophecy' as two of their colleagues are, they believe, unjustly criticized.) The inspectors are introduced together with their special responsibilities and staff with corresponding responsibilities match their introductions by indicating who they are. The stage is set.

The RgI then explains the procedure for grading teachers and the atmosphere changes as people quieten down and serious expressions are maintained. She tells them that by Wednesday the majority of the one and two and six and seven grades will have been awarded. The teachers getting sixes and sevens will be given a verbal warning. If further grades of six and seven are given then a written text will be prepared. It will be confidential to the headteacher and not be available to governors and the person will not be identifiable in the report. In the event that anyone is so graded there will be training opportunities made available to them. She asks if there any questions. There is a silence of about 10 seconds and at this point the inspectors took their leave. (This is not a staff that are backward in coming forward. Their local inspector always expects 'a spirited interchange'). The head then breaks the quietness with a call for Amy to read her Ofsted poem. There are some cries of agreement and some laughter, as some teachers have already heard it, and Amy stands on a chair to declaim it.

'Til We've Done Our Ofsted
Lowstate you need not fear
Though the dreaded Ofsted's here,
Just remember the end is near

And we'll have done our Ofsted.
Lists of what we have to do
Piles of paper just for you.
Have we worries? Just a few!
'Til we've done our Ofsted
Planning folders oh so neat
Act like teaching's such a treat.
No time to sit upon a seat,
'Til we've done our Ofsted
Classroom tidy, great display,
Brilliant lessons everyday.
Of course it's always just this way
'Til we've done our Ofsted
We may feel like tired old hags
Bags so long my whole face sags.
Just grit our teeth . . . I've hit the fags.
'Til we've done our Ofsted
We just need to keep so cool
Smiling sweetly that's the rule.
We must never shout at all
'Til we've done our Ofsted
So when the inspectors they come in
Make sure there's no unruly din,
Give a sincere welcoming grin
'Til we've done our Ofsted
So here it is, it's Ofsted day,
It's not going to go away
But won't it be nice to say
Thank God we've done our Ofsted

During this rendition, focused on by all the teachers round the table, some sitting some standing, except one who busies himself and takes little part, the teachers laugh at the appropriate points and at the end they clap loudly. The poem is ceremoniously pinned to the centre of the notice board and Amy declares, in answer to a question, that it 'only took her five minutes or so for if there's *feeling* it comes easily'. There is loud chatting and amongst this hubbub Laura notices me scribbling quickly and with a glint of humour tempered by the euphoria and tension of the moment she says 'you're just a vulture' and Esther gives me a short diary of her last week. The head then raises her voice above the chatter, and says 'once more into the breech dear friends' and all the teachers begin to leave the staff room for their classrooms, some of them trying to break into singing 'we shall overcome'. With loud laughs and chatter the event has begun.

Chapter 1

Bridging the Gap: The Inspectors' Perspective

We look first at how inspectors viewed their implementation of the inspections. How did inspectors represent and account for their actions? What sense did they make of the inspections they were conducting, and how far does this square with the teachers' experiences? How do we account for any differences? How did they view the emotional trauma suffered by so many teachers? If opposed to such effects, how did they justify their work?

We interviewed all six lead, Registered Inspectors (RgIs) about six months after the actual inspection. We chose to limit ourselves to RgIs because we sought detailed responses, and the RgI is the most important member of the team. They talked to staff prior to inspections, negotiated with the headteacher, appointed and supervised the other inspectors, and wrote the final report. They had to ensure that the standards of the inspection team were maintained and had to make themselves and their material available for inspection by Ofsted itself. All of them worked, at one time, in local government as headteachers or/and advisors or/and inspectors. Simon, Paul and Neil had long experience of inspection with LEAs, while Nathan, Pamela and Chris had less than 10 years in inspection or advisory work at the time of writing. Simon and Nathan still worked as LEA inspectors, while Simon, Neil and Paul had specialized in primary. They were aged between 40 and 55. There were few differences in style and approach to the inspection in general, though each interpreted feedback to the schools differently.

The inspectors, unsurprisingly perhaps, articulate a managerialist discourse. However, there is something else. The inspectors are clearly not just ciphers deploying the Ofsted Framework without question, any more than teachers implement government policy to the full. Nor are they mere technocrats, exercising a total kind of power and control. Nor do they consider themselves infallible or inhuman. The managerialist discourse appears to be mediated through a more humanistic framework, yielding, in part, a kind of 'new' (Newman and Clarke, 1994) or 'humanistic' managerialism, which is more people-centred and where control is modified. We argue that this is how the inspectors resolve the basic contradiction in their structural position between the government and the teachers, and between the technicism of the Ofsted model and their own values. It is how they 'bridge the gap' to their satisfaction — though whether it is to teachers' we shall consider in Chapter 2.

Here, we consider how the RgIs interpret and operationalize the managerialist discourse in which their work is framed, and how they validate their work in the light of this interpretation. We conclude that there are a number of influences at work which contribute to a complex and contradictory picture of the role of inspectors, but which allow them room to develop their own understandings, and to carry out inspections in accordance with their own values and beliefs, which do not altogether accord with managerialism, at least with the rhetoric of it.

Interpreting and Operationalizing a Managerialist Discourse

Our inspectors articulated the well-known features of a managerialist discourse (Ball, 1990a; Wilcox and Gray, 1996), but all in a modified way. In doing so, they illustrate how they perceive these features being operationalized.

Audit

The idea of 'audit' is central to the managerialist discourse, and to the role of Ofsted. It involves the inspection, correction and certification of accounts or activities by qualified and authorized people. Inspections, in fact, are often called 'audits', which are followed by grading information being given to the head and recommendations for improvement. In these respects, schools are no different from commercial enterprises. It implies a neutral procedure, but Power (1994, p. 5) argues that 'far from being passive, audit actively constructs the contexts in which it operates'. How do our inspectors, therefore, see this process? To a considerable extent they clearly do espouse the marketing ideology in which the government's reforms were framed in the late 1980s and early 1990s. Terms such as value for money, documentation, efficiency, effectiveness, standards, investigation, investment, feedback, monitoring, observation, coverage and outcomes are all associated with financial audits and figure prominently in the inspectors' accounts. As in audits, their recommendations often contain terms like grades, judgment, benchmarks, satisfactory, quality assurance, corporate, improvement. But there is a certain modification in their approach.

It is basic to a system of audit that a standardized approach be used, that is that all schools should be seen the same. The concept of audit assumes a common product, a common simple purpose and a common context. Our inspectors subscribed to this to some extent. Neil used the banking metaphor to describe his work:

> I often make comparisons between bank inspectors. They walk through the door and they just say, 'Open your books', nobody worries, it's just a case of 'that's it'. You can't turn round and say, 'you're not looking at

me now', or 'don't come in the staffroom'. It's a case of, 'off you go, I need your room, I need your papers, people as well as figures'. They're all career-oriented people. Absolutely clinical, and nobody worries about it because they accept the accountability aspect. We shouldn't pretend education's so different.

However, in spite of his use of the banking metaphor, Neil also 'wants to consider the context because every school is so very different and really the schools deserve that, they have that right. For me to come in cold and pretend that a middle-class school in a county town in Kent and a Thames-side school are similar, is grossly unfair on the teachers'. In this, he is agreeing with Wragg and Brighouse (1995) who argue that:

> There should be a better Framework for inspection, with certain core features that apply to all schools, as well as options that recognise that primary and secondary, urban and rural, big and small, rich and poor schools are different from each other. The present system assumes that all schools are the same. . . . There is no recognition of different starting points, or of the need to compare like with like. (Ofstin, 1997, p. 24)

In this respect, inspectors are being 'active' in their interpretation of the kind of audit that is required.

Accountability

The process of auditing is underpinned by the notion of accountability. Schools prior to the late 1980s were seen in the managerialist, marketizing ideology as too producer oriented. The emphasis is now strongly on the consumer, and schools have become more accountable to parents and to government. 'Value for money' is one of the main criteria inspectors use. Neil 'looks at everything in society and checks that it is producing value for money. . . . We have no right as teachers to think we have a God-given right to receive money for being pretty mundane or average people'.

It is the same for everybody. Pamela feels that 'everyone should be questioned and be monitored' and that it was now a fact of life. Neil thinks 'the stressed teachers of today will not be the stressed teachers of tomorrow because they will eventually accept it'. Nathan believes that he and his team have 'become accepted within the schools' environments'. They also are accountable to their superiors, and they know what it's like. Neil 'hates being accountable myself, I'll be honest. I worry myself stupid when I get a letter from Ofsted'.

There is an assumption here that the accountability is one way, that is to say that teachers are accountable to inspectors acting as the agents of the government and society. However, according to Neil, this accountability is not the case, and as teachers and schools become more adapted, they will expect more from inspectors in the way of feedback and advice, and make more demands of a good job of inspection from their point of view. Neil was already finding

> during the second round of inspections that there were an awful lot more questions from the teachers and the heads than we had the first round, and I bet people who are inspecting schools under Ofsted on the third inspection they're getting in 10 years, will have to have their act together.

There is a hint of movement here from what might be termed 'hierarchical' to 'mutual accountability'.

Evaluation

Evaluation is a central part of the audit conception. It implies a standard, rational, objective, relentless exercise. Again, while the RgIs recognized its importance, they modified their own approach. Pamela, for example, had

> a lot of work that I must do before the inspection to do justice to the school, and I know that getting it accurate is a dangerous activity. It discredits what the teachers are doing if you do it at a rapid pace, because they spend considerable time above what they normally do to produce the documentation. They're totally committed and they are often producing high quality documents that are practically implemented. They are assessing correctly. They are doing the best they can within financial restraints and time. Then you come in. Wham! An inspection on them, make these judgments, and they've got to live with it when you've gone.

There is acknowledgment here of the merits of, and constraints on, teachers, appreciation of the teachers' perspective, and of the social drama that inspection constitutes for them. The need for evaluation is put within a professional and humanistic frame.

It is similar with observation. Observation is central to the modes of power exerted by managers over the managed. With Ofsted, there is a large element of actual observation, at least in the first instance. The Ofsted Framework demands that inspectors spend 60 per cent of their time observing in classrooms. But is this a matter of validity or control? Foucault might see it as an examination:

> The examination combines the techniques of an observing hierarchy and those of a normalizing judgment. It is a normalizing gaze, a

surveillance that makes it possible to qualify, to classify, and to punish. It establishes over individuals a visibility through which one differentiates and judges them. (Foucault, 1979, p. 175)

Normalizing judgments can be made through use of the standardized framework, which makes available 'an order defined by natural and observable processes' (Foucault, 1979, p. 179).

Our inspectors did not see their observation as surveillance and control. Neil argued that their process of evaluation was more open than that adopted by HMI in the past:

What went before in the old HMI reports was built round mystique and knowing information. You couldn't question that. Have you ever asked an HMI for their CV? We have a history of a very powerful group of people, very clever people, wonderful experience, but really based on great weaknesses like a lack of information, a secret society, a class society.

Furthermore, rather than making cold, analytical, inscrutable judgments kept hidden from teachers, but which would profoundly affect their work and careers, they saw the need for feedback to teachers, though they were not statutorily required to give it. Lack of feedback was seen by teachers as one of the major problems with the first run of Ofsted inspections. For our inspectors, however, it was an integral part of the process of accountability. Nathan observed, 'In primary schools, what we have tended to do is to feed back to the head but we are now building in the element of feeding back to co-ordinators and also to individual classroom teachers.' Feedback also satisfies the desire to be well thought of, 'I suppose if it's going to be a good message, they do want it, they want acclamation.' It was also a 'rights' issue':

I would have thought it's their entitlement really. If you've had someone in your room scribbling about what's going on and about them as well, then I would have thought that ultimately they would want to know what some of the judgments were.

Pamela even notes that for some teachers this is the first time anyone has recognized the worth of their teaching:

What astounds me sometimes is that you tell them good things about their teaching strategies and performance and some teachers say to you, 'No one's told me that before. I didn't know that', and they've had a 20-year teaching experience. I find that awful.

Even where there were time constraints, 'You can have a quick chat with teachers and you can give nods and winks.'

Feedback isn't always accepted by a school, and the tables can be turned on inspectors at times. One of Neil's schools

> posed a very serious problem for me because the governors chose to reject Ofsted. When I'd finished the feedback to the Governing Body they all sat in stony silence. At the end of it the Chairman said 'I need to speak to you', and then he gave me a seven page letter of everything I'd done wrong in his view. He wrote to Ofsted and I had all hell for months trying to sort it out. I had to spend days summarizing all the things we'd done and I got a little letter from Ofsted saying, 'in all bar some minority little points, everything that you have said is correct and the governors were wrong', but that's how extreme it can be, and it's very upsetting.

While feedback can be an interactive device for improved teaching, it can also be an important resource to the head in the micropolitics of the school (Ball, 1990a), reinforcing the hierarchy at the next level in relation to the level below that:

> Some heads are flabbergasted when I offer this but every single one has accepted, and why? This is the empowerment of the head. I feedback to the teachers on the strengths and weaknesses. And then I go to the head and I say it to the head and the head can then use that information. So it allows the head to grow and develop. (Neil)

Inspectors may even be asked to break the bad news to a teacher by the head teacher who wishes to retain a different relationship with his or her staff. Neil, for example, was asked by a head to tell a teacher about her poor report. However, in some cases feedback is done with an element of negotiation, indicating a collegial element. Neil presents a draft report to the head and they go through it together. He tells the head,

> 'We'll work on it and I'll make notes on what you say, and then I'll come back and you get another copy'. I do everything I humanly can. I don't change it if it's right, but I will listen to what the head says.

However, individual feedback to teachers can be a nightmare for inspectors in a large school. On one occasion, Neil thought he could have a heart attack, 'because when I've been through a couple of very heavy feedback sessions I'm shaking. Oh, I'm in a terrible state!'

Inspectors clearly are human beings who themselves are subject to trauma and stress if they step too far outside the Framework. But some humanizing of the process is important to them as HMCI has recently recognized, 'It is inhumane for an inspector to come in and listen, and leave without offering comment' (Barnard, 1997).

We have here, therefore, more openness, more feedback, more negotiability, more sensitivity than might be expected from a rigid application of the Framework. This is carried further in the idea of self-review. The basic aim of the managerialist orientation is to bring schools up to recognition and appreciation of the benchmarks, so that ultimately they can control themselves, in other words become their own 'experts'. In the managerialist image, this would be in relation to *external* targets. Ball (1990a, p. 162) argues that 'teachers are trapped into taking responsibility for their own 'disciplining' through schemes of self-appraisal, school improvement, and institutional development. He might now add 'Ofsted inspections' to the list. Self-management is a kind of 'steering at a distance' (Kickert, 1991), where the success of management is 'proportional to its ability to hide its own mechanisms' (Foucault, 1979, p. 86). This is typical of what Foucault calls 'disciplinary' power which is operated through its invisibility and normalizing technologies of the self (as opposed to more traditional forms of power that are visible, shown and manifested). Yet while the power is invisible, the subjects are highly visible, if not in inspections, in their results, and the constant possibility of inspection if there is any deviation from normality. As Hartley (1994, p. 235) notes, there may appear a basic contradiction here between central strategic control and local management. But not if the local management assumes the same discourse as central government.

Self review for our inspectors is not altogether dependent on that condition. Simon feels that inspections help schools to be actively independent rather than slaves to external forces, since they are

> certainly making schools look at what they're doing. I think it's getting schools to look at the roles different people are playing within it and it's challenging as to whether governors know enough about their schools. From these points of view I think it's a good thing. The latest talk is about self review and I think there's a lot going for that . . . Self review would go back to the school aims and you might say 'I'm going to ensure independent activities by pupils. What's that going to look like? How am I going to see that when I walk round? Or is it just another phrase from another handbook of somebody else's down the road'.

However, the ambivalence of the inspectors' position comes out in other statements. Nathan, for example, feels that inspections are about:

> School improvement, raising standards of achievements, that's what it's about ultimately, for the kids, providing schools with benchmarks from which they can develop. So it's really informing them, helping to inform their development priorities. One of the schools where the inspection went down well, was one where she (headteacher) said she felt it was 'almost like getting external consultancy in terms of where we're at'. She now wanted to re-affirm that 'we're right at our position where we are and where we need to go to' . . . In the past we

only addressed staff meetings, we didn't get into classrooms and this helps us focus more on the implementation of the school's policies . . . You can say this is 'big brother' but schools do need improving and there's always been inspections.

Here are the 'benchmarks', the external targets, the 'informing', and the view that if self-review does not go in the right direction, 'the expert, the authority, the consultant, the moral disciplinarian is at hand to intervene' (Ball, 1990b, p. 163). Nathan's reference to 'big brother' could be apt, for in Orwell's '1984' the mass of the population acquiesced in being controlled by 'big brother'. In the case of teachers, such acquiescence might involve a sacrifice of some basic values and amount to what has been described as 'misrecognized profession-alism' (Densmore, 1987).

Quality Assurance

The same ambivalence applies to the matter of quality assurance. Basic questions are *whose* quality, on what criteria does it rest, and how is it secured? Is it achieved through distance and monitoring (managerialism), or close working with teachers and teacher development (professionalism)? Is judgment based on the authority and expertise of the inspectors during the inspection week, or the maximum of evidence available? Both sets of views were evident in inspectors' responses.

Chris felt there had to be a system that allowed teachers to know that they were very poor, and for their headteachers to know that too. The inspector's assessment should then be used to improve that teacher as a matter of urgency. Where they marked teachers as 'very good', he thought that helped to raise the quality of teaching because that showed the management of the school what makes a really good teacher. Before Ofsted, they were much more subjective and woolly about that. Now they were much more analytical.

However, the detailed information that goes into the analysis is gathered through their own devices. Pamela was shocked to receive a recommendation from Ofsted that they look at the minimum of paperwork:

If I'm doing my job properly and the team members are doing their job properly, they will have received pre-inspection, documents and profiles, which give a lot of information. Again I'm astonished with Ofsted who say the 'minimum of information'. I think we should give as much information as possible to the inspectors in our teams. The subject coordinator should feel that I know what I'm at.

Neil agreed with this:

The reason to know the school is so the staff believe that we're there not as nasty executioners but have made an effort to come to terms with them. There's nothing worse than sitting in front of a teacher and not knowing the documentation well. What indicators of credibility are you giving the teacher? You've got to know that, you've got to know the background that the school gives you.

There are differences between the independent RgIs and the LEA inspectors' approaches to their definitions of quality assurance. In most cases the Ofsted team arrive as unknown inspectors who carry out what appears to be an objective role and after reporting, they leave, never to be seen again. In fact the independent RgIs are keen to show that as part of their quality assurance they do not tout for advisory work after an inspection. However the LEA RgIs, whilst maintaining a distance from the school, feel that the LEA contact assists quality assurance. Nathan feels

> it's far less valuable when you've not got too much in common, never met each other before, you do the inspection and then clear off. I found a report quite difficult to write when I had to join one of these teams. It didn't strike me as being particularly consistent overall. So what I'm saying is if you're going to do it, I think you need people who are committed to using it in a developmental way, as developmental as it can be and at the same time if you've got the same consistent systems, I think it can work.

Nathan thus does not agree with the Ofsted training which suggests that evaluations, though they may indeed be individually subjective, are effectively moderated by discussions in the team. He also argues that working in the same LEA in which you inspect schools can lead to a more developmental approach to inspection:

> An Ofsted inspection is very much monitoring, it is not into the developmental side. However, the developmental side comes if you're getting on well with the school and you can start talking to them. You can say, 'If I was you I'd try this, I can try that.' That's an informal way, but the responsibility for the advisory support rests with LEA, and the LEA needs different prongs of attack. It needs an inspection service. You've got to be able to report standards in your own borough and then you need an advisory report service which is working alongside teachers in schools. The more Ofsted is driven by people who need to earn a living by doing just Ofsted, the more they are packing in Ofsted after Ofsted, the less effective can the school's development be. I do the developmental supporting because I want to go there, I want to do a good job. There's the opportunity to talk to people and say 'I'm finding this because of this and this, this is my judgment' and get them to be involved in the process. You get something from it, you enjoy it, you go there to see positive things. If you go in there and think I've got to

knock this out by the end of this week and I've got to do the preparation for the next one the week after, you're not going to get the same quality.

Nathan appears to be agreeing here with the chair of the Ofstin assessors, who records, 'Inspection under its provisions is also deliberately *external*, in the sense that nobody with an internal knowledge of the institution is admitted to the team. Conversely, no member of the team is allowed to work with the school and its governors on how best to put recommendations into practice. That may be good for accountability, but it is most unlikely to be good for school improvement' (Ofstin, 1997, p. 30).

However, whilst inspectors believe that most teachers want to do their best not only in inspections but professionally, there is still, they feel, a necessity for supervision. Most of the teachers Pamela feels

> will try and provide the very best they can for the children but continual surveillance is necessary to ensure that it is rigorous and there is a standard, a bench mark. Someone from outside is insurance of a quality, judgment statements, investigation.

The credentials of the outside person rests on their knowledge and expertise. But is this being used as a form of power, to control schools and teachers, or as professional aid to teacher development? The development of the expert is a central feature of power relations according to Foucault. Ball (1990b, pp. 156–7) argues 'Management is a . . . discourse which allows its speakers and its incumbents to lay exclusive claims to certain sorts of expertise . . . and to a set of procedures that casts others, subordinates, as objects of that discourse and the recipients of those procedures, whether they wish to be or not.'

Again, our inspectors profess a bit of each. 'Expertise' figures prominently in their comments. Paul felt that inspectors had an advantage over headteachers through inspecting lots of primary schools over a period of years, working across the country with different people in different groups. Headteachers, by contrast, may have spent a considerable amount of time in primary education but only in a few schools. Neil emphasized how his experience was valued by Ofsted, 'I didn't do the Reggie test for Primary. I did the two day conversion and they said I had such a depth of experience from my inspections, in working for a local authority, that I didn't have to do it, and I was very privileged and honoured at the time.' The National Curriculum, he feels, requires specialist knowledge:

> Your team can't have a lot of primary heads on the team because they don't have the expertise, they don't have the subject knowledge. If I want to test a primary head on any subject other than English, they will fail. The standards of attainment of the children and the progress they make in the areas of the National Curriculum is the prime focus of the Ofsted inspection, that's what the Framework is written for.

Consequently, the RgIs look to fill their teams with specialists in subject areas, Key Stages and Early Years experience, otherwise 'you don't have the qualitative discussion necessary to make judgments' (Paul).

Legitimation

From a managerialist perspective, the inspectors' position rests on legal authority. For the inspectors, however, the basic justification for their position, and the main reason why all should be accountable, lies not with any abstract theories of control by the State, but with the pupils. Paul was happy for it to be what he called a 'cooperative engagement' with the school 'until the point that it seems that the children are not first and foremost in everybody's mind and so it's an equal opportunities issue'. The RgIs emphasized that their main focus was to ensure that pupils were receiving a satisfactory education, and they all drew on their own life experiences. Chris's teacher at school was 'bloody awful'. He felt sure that many children were 'getting a raw deal', that made him 'upset'. He went into teaching to do something for children. He thought he 'helped' a bit as a teacher, even more as a headteacher. But, 'Since being an inspector I've done a hell of a lot more for more children than anyone does as a headteacher.' In Paul's Welsh mining community, he was top of the class, but when he moved to the town, he was put in a remedial group. There was no consistency of practice between the schools, and no equal opportunity for children of similar ages. Nathan said, 'It's about kids, some schools need moving on.' Neil was passionate in his belief that 'if you ever lose sight of children you should be cast aside, cut off, have your Reggie status removed'. He had seen some of his four children 'taken to pieces' by teachers for a whole year, with heads replying to complaints with 'platitudes', or with other considerations in mind, such as 'Yes I can always weed her out but will I get an applicant?'

Much of the talk about pupils is based in support for those from disadvantaged areas. Pamela had been in a primary school,

> where the social circumstances are very similar to an inner city school but two of the inspectors refused to acknowledge that. They saw nice housing in the area and were condemning the school and I had quite a hard time to stop that school from being considered as being a school at risk. . . . They were giving a very good education to those children, but the independent school inspector wouldn't recognize that these children come with different social skills for a start. The school had to work very hard on getting those children to respond, respect each other as well as adults and interrogate with each other.

RgIs are now asked to take the social priority of the school into account, and 'you can comment more on in terms of the characteristics of the school'. However, Pamela notes that, 'although you may comment, the SATs results are in the league table and put beside others. There's no getting away with that at all. That's as raw as it comes'.

All this, of course, accepts the model of 'satisfactory education' enshrined in the National Curriculum and national assessment. As expressed, with emphasis on the pupils, it is a position that the teachers in our study would also strongly support. Even so, it might be argued that Neil's philosophy is turned into a technical one. The children's success and happiness are to be judged by their progress through the hoops of the National Curriculum and national assessment:

> My basic philosophy is that I want the children to get the best possible deal and that's not a euphemism. I want them to be happy, enjoy school and you know 99 per cent of schools, 99 per cent of children are very happy, but I also want them to have good life chances and that means being successful and being successful means attaining, understanding, learning, appreciating not just in English, Maths and Science but across the whole range.

In summary, the inspectors subscribe to a complex mixture of two discourses which are polar opposites in some respects:

Managerialist Discourse	*Professional/Developmental Discourse*
• View schools the same	• View schools differently
• Hierarchical accountability	• Mutual accountability
• Passive auditing	• Active auditing
• Objective evaluation	• Subjective evaluation
• Observation as control	• Observation as aid to validity
• Systematic grading	• Negotiative feedback
• External targets	• Internal targets
• Authoritative quality control	• Developmental quality assurance
• Expertise as power	• Expertise as aid to professionalism
• Legal authority	• Moral authority

Validation

A similar ambivalence attends the inspectors' approach to validity. Ofsted inspections have been strongly criticized on these grounds. Wilcox and Gray (1996) note that the guiding Ofsted Handbook 'presents with great magisterial confidence an analysis of the school in terms of apparently self-evident structures and outcomes (p. 67)'. There are assumptions that there is *a* school reality, that it is knowable, and can be represented in the inspectors' report. In effect, of course, the inspectors' report is one representation of a school reality as mediated through the theoretical assumptions of the managerialist discourse. Other representations are possible and potentially equally, if not more, valid (see Henkel, 1991). Gilroy and Wilcox (1997) argue that many Ofsted judgments cannot be value neutral, and that their criteria of judgment have no broad agreement. Fitz-Gibbon and Stephenson (1996) feel that 'Ofsted's methods have failed to meet minimally acceptable standards' (p. 16) in this respect. According to the headteachers she consulted, most of the lessons seen by inspectors were unrepresentative of normality, and samples were inadequate. The limited judgments and descriptions given could not possible match the wide variety of expedience encountered, even within a single school. Too little account was taken of differences between schools in terms of catchment area and pupil intake. And notions of what constitutes 'good practice' could be 'a shared prejudice rather than accurate knowledge' (p. 17). There have been other trenchant criticisms (see, for example, Wilcox and Gray, 1996, pp. 70–8).

However, a managerialist discourse would have little regard for criteria of validity as practised by educational researchers. The latter have come under strong attack from managerialists, who claim that researchers have used such criteria as a mask for a disguised ideology — one strongly at variance with the recent reforms, including that that has established Ofsted. Ofsted's warrant for making judgments is based in expertise, experience, knowledge, and authority. A research discourse, by contrast, would lay emphasis on evidence, rigorously acquired through long and detailed research; scrupulous methods; triangulation; and respondent validation. There were elements of both of these models in the inspectors' responses. These responses revolve around three sets of opposites:

1   Standardization and sameness v flexibility and difference
2   External v internal reality
3   Personal v universal criteria of judgment.

We examine each in turn.

Standardization and Sameness v Flexibility and Difference

Team Matters

The inspectors did not consider themselves perfect. They were mindful of a number of problems that affected the quality of their work. Members of the inspection team are expected to be similarly trained and each member therefore is able to make similar, and reliable judgments. The team also is meant to provide the forum for discussion of evaluations. However, the practice varies from the principle. This is unfortunate, since, as Pamela notes,

> If you work with teams together it's an advantage because you know how they operate and how they work. If you're working with someone you've never worked with before they're unknown to you in all sorts of ways, how they operate, how they may or may not ask questions of

staff and upset them because that does happen. They're very reliant on each other.

In some cases teams do not meet until the first day of the inspection. Chris has 'not yet done an inspection where I've known anyone'.

With the Framework and general agreement about model and aims, one might assume inspectors were all of one view, representing a common baseline. This is not the case, according to Pamela. She admits to struggles within the inspection team over refusals to use the comparative material provided and over her more deeply held values:

> I've been on teams where you have people from independent schooling backgrounds, and they are inspecting the state system. I come with my own baggage as well, I admit that too, but they will have different standards of what's acceptable for behaviour, what children can do and should be able to do by a certain age and they find that they get challenged when you have inspection meetings.

A further team problem is that of balance in relation to knowledge and experience of what is being examined. Many teams have put the emphasis on subject knowledge, and left themselves short of expertise in the primary, and particularly Early Years areas. It is also difficult to live up to the aims of the 'greatest expertise' and the 'highest standards' in terms of team recruitment. RgIs find themselves stuck with the problem of hiring the appropriate quality of inspectors in a competitive context with limited resources. Paul thought

> The playing field is not level. Some LEA teams cut their costs and we're based in the South East, the most competitive area — that means it's very difficult to invest in that quality.

Task Problems

All the areas that are judged appear to be given the same value both in the inspection and in the report. The time available does not match the task prescribed. Simon, for example, reports

> you get things like 'links with parents and outside agencies' alongside 'Special Educational Needs (SEN)'. . . . Links with parents are important but there's only so much you can do on that to find it out. Whereas SEN is two days' investigation at least for one person.

The equal value given to a large range of a school's activities can mean that criticism of a minor part of the school contributes to general critical evaluations of the school. The brevity of the inspectors' visit affects other judgments. According to Nathan, 'It's difficult to know how to assess good consistent teaching against excellent performances put on during the inspection week. It seems unfair not to award top grades to consistent performers.' Another problem is being both critical and laudatory. Nathan argues that 'there are ways of writing things up that show differences between the judgments, but sometimes good teaching is obscured in a poor report on a Key Stage and vice-versa'.

There is a further problem over imprecise aims. Pamela has been on teams where they all say 'I'm not really sure what I am looking for here and what the real purpose of this exercise is', and she has been guilty of it herself. You may have 'various prompt sheets' but 'beyond that, there's not the actual clarity of what you're looking for, whilst you're looking through the pupils' work'.

Inspectors are required to make a number of evaluations at a time in lessons that may have variable sections or phases:

> It's selective. . . . Do you focus on those children that are really achieving well, that are well motivated, that are on task, whether they understand what they're doing, or do you focus on the group that is slightly off task, they've finished their work but they're not quite sure what to do. Ideally you focus on all of those things, and it's all under one form, but then you've got the task of the teaching grade. What's the quality of learning for the grade? What's the progress for the grade? Because you've got one group that's achieving really well and you've got another group that's not achieving to their potential. (Pamela)

Such a practice is 'open to all sorts of personal interpretations and mis-interpretations and mis-judgments. As you go through the process you have certain things that we all latch on to and look for and other things perhaps get passed over and we miss things'. Consistency and correlation between inspectors' judgments is thus missing.

Freedom and Flexibility

In general the inspectors have relished a new found freedom (though this is less so for the LEA inspectors) which permits them to be more flexible than they were before. Thus, far from feeling constrained by their position in the new managerialist hierarchical structure, the reverse was the case. Chris felt he became independent on becoming a RgI. When working for a LEA he

> had to go for meetings regularly about reorganization, restructuring, and we kept restructuring for all kinds of reasons. So that was absolutely awful. The public money that was wasted by meeting after meeting after meeting! I was absolutely bored.

This freedom from bureaucracy seems to have given many of them a new lease of life. They have more room for manoeuvre and negotiation:

I refine the Ofsted process as much as I can. There's no actual bureaucracy as such . . . The local authority inspectors are prima donnas in a
way. They complain busily about their work load — three inspections
per term — but as an independent person I'm doing at least five a
term. But they couldn't possibly manage that number because of all
the meetings they have to go to . . . the demands are too great.

Pamela enjoyed the diversity of roles in her LEA post, but

didn't enjoy the political intervention and working to other people's
deadlines all the time. For me (the new system) suits my domestic
needs because a lot of the time I can work at home if I so choose. I
can take on as much or as little work as I choose.

Neil also felt newly empowered. The LEA had started to question the last
inspection he had done, but had stopped when they realized that 'the LEA
expertise in primary education was so much lower than my seven inspectors
. . . they couldn't dream of arguing. They had two or three primary inspectors,
some primary advisors working right across the LEA. I had seven people
totally immersed, you couldn't argue.' Neil never wanted to go back to that
system.

In terms of the Ofsted Framework, Paul wanted it to be both flexible and
standardized:

If the Framework does not enable inspectors to applaud good teaching
even in the context where standards may be lower than expected for
the age and ability range and the progress in individual lessons is not
great, then that seems a shame.

However, 'I think if the framework is implemented effectively across the nation
then all schools should be receiving the same sort of inspection approach and
it should be developmental and it shouldn't be making staff desperately nervous, it should contribute to long term development.' He also thought it was not
prescriptive and needed to be interpreted:

The Ofsted Framework isn't demanding a focus on certain interpretations of management nor is it demanding that there's a particular
approach in the classroom or that there is a particular subject based
emphasis. The interpretation of the framework rests on the people in
whose hand the inspection is laid.

Chris agrees, but thinks that people can interpret it too literally, and that 'some
head teachers get bees in their bonnets and interpret it in a very rigid way,
which is nonsense'.

However, Simon thought the frame too narrow:

> Schools are about the moral, social, personal development path as well as the curriculum subjects. People have found those difficult to inspect but. . . . You want Ofsted to be able to take into account that, for example, '90 per cent of the children in our primary schools go on school journeys, that they've got a library, that every child will learn to swim, every child will have the opportunity to learn a musical instrument, that we have a choir, we have an orchestra, we do a lot of school games; we have wheelchair access or on average we have 20 parents working in our school'. . . . They don't come under a neat heading you see. At the moment Ofsted focuses too much.

Nevertheless the RgIs generally supported the Framework and don't feel 'it was foisted upon' them. 'It's part of the job; it's part of the national framework so you end up doing it. I think you can do it as humanely as possible.' (Nathan). However, they all felt that that they had to interpret the framework and bring their experience and expertise to the situation. This was exemplified by their interpretation as to how to implement grading guidelines. Pamela implemented the guidelines according to her reasoning. For example, they were supposed to tell teachers their grades on the day they were inspected, but Pamela delayed till the last day, because 'if you tell them on day one, they're going to be totally demoralized and that could throw the inspection. Their performance could well go down and continue on a downward spiral.' Nathan also thought 'It's not very helpful if it's going to come out destroying the teacher without doing all you can to validate a judgment.'

External v Internal Reality

The inspectors are aware that there are a range of issues connected with the reality, or realities, upon which they base their judgments, but they still show an ambivalent response.

Time Problems

They recognize the 'snapshot' scenario:

> We've got three days of your entire school year that we're looking at and the focus of three days only. So we'll make comment on what we see. If there's evidence of documentation, other forms of evidence where things obviously take place, we can comment on those as well. But if we haven't seen those, or we haven't seen it in paper form or in implementation during the three days, we can't comment on it. The

school has to recognize that we're in for three days only. It's very much a snapshot.

At times in the inspectors' comments that does not seem a problem. The RgIs believe it is crucial to distance themselves from the context. The managerialist model would require this to distinguish managers from managed, and to retain their sense of hierarchy and power, considered necessary to achieve their ends. Thus, Pamela is concerned that a longer relationship with a school would affect her subjectivity, and she prefers the shorter acquaintance as an aid to distance and objectivity. She echoes some of the concerns of qualitative researchers, but comes to different conclusions, since researchers would favour the longer time period and seek other aids to analytical distance. But this is inspection, not research:

> If you have a longer relationship with the school, some of your judg-ments could be compromised. If you go in there prepared, you've got questions to ask and answers to get. You've got your debating with other inspectors, we'll challenge each other and you should come out with the right judgments. If in doubt you've got to go back and test them out on the teacher and the headteacher wherever the evidence is lacking. If you do it over a longer period I think you run the risk of building a better relationship and you could compromise some of the judgments and some of the evidence because you're more familiar with the school and you don't really want to say such things.

Gilroy and Wilcox (1997) argue that with the conventional criteria employed by Ofsted, 'the subtleties of inter-personal relationships are being crudely ignored' (p. 35). Pamela seems to be saying that this is a complexity she does not wish to get into. The snapshot is not only good enough, it enables 'right judgments' to be made. But her views are not as clear cut as this. Pamela admits that in such a short period there may be school aspects they may not be able to uncover. 'Often you feel you would like to be a fly on the wall to know what it was really like or what really happened. There are some things that really irritate you but you just cannot get underneath, you cannot get behind and beyond, you know there's something there but you cannot pin it down so you have to leave it.' The professional discourse sits side by side with the managerialist:

> I think it's very difficult to do what you have to do in three days not because you don't work quickly or anything like that; it's almost an impossible task. Personally, I would never undertake a two day inspec-tion or a two team member inspection because again I think it's not enough to get accurate judgments. Although you get the documents from the inspectors, they don't always write as much as you need to ensure you've got the accurate judgments. You can phone them up but they're probably on another inspection. So you can't contact them for three weeks.

The inspectors value comparisons with each other. But Pamela's comment also shows the problems of short, one-off visits:

> A colleague came out of a lesson and asked me to go in because she was concerned about equal opportunities. On the mat were two boys and one girl, boys tracking the duplo around the mat, in the home corner there were three girls cooking party food for a boy. So I went in less than five minutes later. There were more girls than boys playing duplo on the mat and building things. In terms of the construction toys, it was all girls, in terms of the home corner there was something like three boys all dressed up in party frocks with necklaces and hats on cooking. You couldn't have had more opposites and that's what can happen if you are not allowed enough time to investigate properly.

If there is so little time, there may not be an opportunity to validate observations like the one above:

> You haven't got firm evidence. You can't make judgments, it's too soon, too early and you don't have the time, even in the feedback, you don't have the time to talk and discuss at length.

She, like most of the inspectors, reports back to postholders at the end of the third or fourth day:

> The judgments you make have to be totally secure. Any judgment you make can be challenged and if you haven't got a good sound evidence base it has to go. You can't risk saying anything that is not secure. However, you haven't much time for reflection. It's as good as you're going to get on this model. It could be improved yes, but the inspection process could be improved.

Pamela recognizes the need for firm evidence, and the limitations of the Ofsted model. What they have is a compromise — unsurprisingly given the mix of discourses.

Analytical Distance or Close Relationships?

The inspectors did not feel that distance should be achieved in a cold, analytic manner. Pamela, for example, thought 'a distance is necessary but at the same time you've got be human when you go in there.' Neil agreed: 'You go in, you speak to the head, you have a chat to them, you try and form what I'd call a professional link — I'm not a friend, but it's a professional link.' Chris feels he does a better job being more distanced than an LEA inspector can be:

> I wouldn't be able to inspect as thoroughly if I was in an advisory role. Every day of the week would be doing something different within the school. If I had to spend my time as an advisor as well, it would be me

who'd have to pick up the pieces and put them all together again. Putting it together is a full time job in itself.

You have to have an independent body of inspectors, according to Chris, because 'advisors' who work for the local authority

don't watch children learning properly; they've either got stuck in the headteacher's office for hours or having a tour of the school and all that stuff. They are distracted. They have a tour of the school and you see what's on the walls but they've never actually sat in a classroom and watched the teachers. They would then say 'It's a very nice little school.'

No doubt Simon and Nathan, the LEA inspectors, would disagree with him. Simon works for an LEA and inspects the LEA's schools. He argues for a closer connection with schools in order to enhance development, as we heard earlier, but he also maintains some distance and feels that this is a way of getting at the truth:

The school that you met me in, I'd only been in there once and that was about four years ago. So that was fair that I led that inspection. . . . So, we do keep a distance. We hope that our knowledge locally doesn't change our judgment; it's just realistic what the situation is in the schools and this adds a credibility to it.

Neil ensures distance as a RgI by not taking responsibility for evaluating the management of the school so that he can report to the head teacher objectively:

It's fundamental because when you feed back to the head, you feed back to the head at a personal level. If a colleague's written it, you've just got to say, 'Well this is what's been found and this is my evidence. Do please argue with me because I'll check my colleague's evidence.' So you're intervening in that one-to-one relationship and at the same time it allows you to make the judgment.

The RgIs value distance for objectivity and familiarity for easing the atmosphere.

Contaminated or Uncontaminated Data?

The inspectors recognize that there is contamination of the field by the inspection process (see Chapter 3, and Fitz-Gibbon, 1996). Pamela is sure that less creative teaching goes on during the inspection:

You don't often see it, and you know why you don't often see it, because you would probably do exactly the same. You'll go for the formalities and procedures and you'll go for the safe secure teaching strategies. And you know that they're doing it. You get very cross that you can't interfere with what you're seeing and what's going on. You've got to judge on what you're seeing there. But you might talk with them afterwards, about what they usually do. It wouldn't even help if HMCI were to suggest teachers work as creatively as possible in an inspection. They won't do it and I'm sure they won't because there is a risk element there and the risk is that sometimes when you do exciting, interesting, different things, children react very differently, not always the way you would want them to act if you're being inspected. They could appear to be undisciplined, off task. It's definitely crappy what's happening. It's going for the same approach all the time. Sometimes you do come across lessons where just by nature they're stimulating and exciting. And the teachers are fantastic.

Simon admits that 'You know that during the inspection you are going to inhibit the performance of people running over a whole day, unless you are well organized and unless it's part of what you normally do it will expose itself, it will show. It will show by the behaviour of the children.' However, the children we spoke to were well aware of joining in the performance, 'All the naughty children weren't that naughty this week, they were quite good' (Ben, Year 5).

There is a requirement for the inspection team to take into account 'value added' criteria but as Nathan argues 'It is up to the school to present you with ways in which the school has added value to the pupil's learning by showing you past and present differences in say arts appreciation or reading levels.' This leaves it more open to a RgI as to whether they encourage schools to do this, as Simon does:

Well it's not built into Ofsted but it perhaps should be a little more explicit. I can see schools feeling negatively about an inspection and not offering anything but there's another opportunity to highlight the particular things that are really good about the school. Why not show your orchestra off? They might have been doing a performance a week later, why not let them do it that week so that you can see it.

However, comparisons are made by Ofsted teams of achievement levels of different pupils at different Key Stages. Nathan acknowledged this about the inspection of a secondary school: 'We tested year 6 and year 11 in the week we were in and showed improvement in their achievement levels, but I suppose you're right — they were different pupils.' Similarly, SATs results from different years in primary schools are used as performance indicators.

Personal v Universal Criteria of Judgment

Personal Expertise

Inspectors place great faith in their judgmental expertise, which they feel enables them to penetrate to the essence of a school, sometimes through layers that obscured the truth. Some schools may think they are good enough and not realize the possibilities. In such cases, the inspectors' report might not be welcomed, might cause upset and anger, but might nonetheless be necessary. Chris was amazed 'how much wool they pull over parents' eyes'. He gave as an example

> a beautiful little village school, beautiful uniform they had, their teacher had been there a few years; they were all very comfortable. We went in and said that they've got serious weaknesses. You never know until you're in the classroom, when you dig in deep to see exactly what they are doing. Superficially they look lovely at school, but when you actually watch teachers teaching, watch children learning you find out. The headteacher was devastated; the chair of governors was absolutely incensed, and sent for me for my feedback. 'I know what you're going to say, and I'll tell you now that we don't accept a word of it!' She said, 'You've stabbed us in the back.'

They are convinced that they get to the reality of the school situation:

> At the end of the day the report is about the standards achieved and that's what you're judging it on when you're there, regardless of what they've done, whatever they've put up on the wall, because you listen to a child read, you look at their writing while they're writing it and the teachers can't do that for the children. (Simon)

To support these judgments, they gather evidence through observation, field notes, documentation and interviews with teachers, parents and pupils. As they do this, they interpret the material and then make a judgment. The judgment is based on experience of schools and commonly understood qualitative terms such as progress, attitude, involvement, independence — though these still have to be interpreted. Quantitative measurements are also carried out, for example, numerical counts of specific equipment, test results and comparisons of achievement with national norms. The judgment is then supported by some form of evidence on forms that are not open to public scrutiny but are kept secret from all but Ofsted members. Part of the evidence may be validated by another inspector's observations and the judgment adjusted. Interpretations are also made of the procedures of an inspection. All the judgments are then gathered together by the RgI who constructs the report.

However, the inspectors laid claim to more personal criteria that aided their decision-making. For example, they sometimes used the self as a yardstick. Simon believes his experience as a teacher and an inspector who has visited lots of schools is a basis for judgment, 'It's your own knowledge, isn't it, of what you know and expect the children should be able to do. You know as a teacher, when you used to teach first year juniors, or year 3.' Nathan admitted he was personally involved:

Your feelings are engaged because you're making judgments, you constantly turn it over in your head — there's a high level of responsibility in terms of whether you're giving a teachers a 'satisfactory or better' or something which is verging on your satisfaction. You don't particularly like giving them but ultimately you have to reinforce the Ofsted objectives and say, 'Look, is it or isn't it?' Basically the question I like to ask myself is 'Could you do it better? What could you do to that would make it better?'

At other times, he resorted to ideas of 'worthwhileness': 'From all the evidence you've got, is this teacher producing something which is worthwhile, and is she doing all the things that are required to do that?' Alternatively, Neil used children as his measure: 'When you look at a teacher, you don't say, "I can do that, I'm better than that", you come in and you say, "Does it promote the children or not?"'. Pamela goes by

> instinct I think. I haven't got a particular model. I have to know that the National Curriculum is in place. That the strategy requirements are met. That day to day secure environments are provided. That all those things such as social, personal education, all those are in place, the children feel happy and secure and that there's a good stable learning environment. But as to the actual teaching in the class, as long as it's effective, the children are learning, making gains in knowledge, consolidating new learning. It has to be right.

Paul argues that subjective judgments are not negative, but soundly based on experience and expertise. He draws a parallel with the medical profession. 'You wouldn't say of someone who has years and years of experience of examining that they medically make a subjective judgment of somebody. You'd say they'd make a professional judgment.' Hammersley (1997, p. 14), however, argues that this analogy is suspect, since 'it seems likely that much medical research avoids many of the problems that face educational researchers, in particular those deriving from the social world. . . . Similarly, medical practice may generally be closer to the technical rather than to the practical end of the spectrum'.

The independent RgIs claim neutrality as an aid to validity. Paul is concerned about the problem of educational ideologies which he perceives as dominating LEA inspection teams:

> When we win our contract, we've got no axe to grind; we walk through the door and they'll often say 'Thank God it's a new group, we don't want our in-house crew.' They don't want the in-house crew, if they're honest. They won't say that publicly because most schools are LEA and because they're frightened of the knock-on political effects. They'll actually turn round and say, 'We don't want the East Sussex view, we

don't want the Kent view, we don't want the Bexley view, we don't want the Greenwich view, we want someone who's been in them all and gives an overview.' I say 'The greatest strength we bring to you is we have no prejudices; I don't know you; you don't know me' and I give them on the first morning, a little aide-mémoire and it lists the names of the inspectors in the team and it says, 'If you know any of these please tell us.'

The attack on LEAs is interesting, especially as they featured strongly as government targets in the 1980s and early 1990s. They were seen as politically motivated, while Paul claims that he is completely neutral. The latter is demonstrably not the case, as he is operating a politically loaded model. The claim is symptomatic, once more, of inspectors holding to a perception of a 'naive reality' (Hammersley, 1992), further endorsed by their belief that they can 'suspend' certain beliefs.

Simon, for example, who does work for a local authority, feels that such work is not a problem and would argue that knowing the school assists in faster development. He agrees that he supports particular practices, but that he is not hidebound by them:

For example, I have a personal view that they should have a wider access to books etc., etc., but if they're using 13 colour coded books and the child can read with accuracy, fluency or whatever it is, then it goes down as a successful lesson. However, I may feel that they're not being stretched because they're not exposed to a wider range of books. I might see queues round the teacher's desk, now my gut reaction is 'that's not good', but I've got to go and see if it is. It might be that the teacher is explaining one thing to one child and the other children can pick up something from what she is saying. I'd have to make a judgment as to whether that was good or not. I've got to judge on what's happening in the room. It's like rows and rows of sums isn't it, if they don't get anything else you say they're getting a narrow range of experience. I don't use worksheets myself, but I will go on and see why they use a worksheet on this occasion. A worksheet in itself needn't be a bad thing because they might be practising something; it might be a way of testing or evaluating.

Neil is more convinced that prejudice can be eradicated with time and that it is possible to separate expertise from personal pedagogic beliefs:

The first point is that we force the team members to leave their prejudices and their philosophies and everything at the door. The hardest thing that an inspector does is to do the first 10 inspections because they've got all the prejudices of their own experiences and they need to leave those behind. You must come in and be very highly criteria referenced.

The assumption here again is that these 'criteria' are neutral, factual and object-ive and having general agreement. Gilroy and Wilcox (1997), on the contrary, have shown the criteria involved in the Ofsted approach to be tacitly situated within certain conventions and having no guarantee of broad agreement though they are made to appear as if they do.

Universal Criteria

Together with the more personal criteria, the inspectors deploy more universal criteria, that is those more generally recognized as aids to validity. Prominent among these are collaboration, with some respondent validation, and various kinds of triangulation.

Collaboration

Inspectors preferred to work on a collegial basis with teachers — but it was a conditional one:

> So as far as I'm concerned, with all the heads and all the staff who I've talked to it's stressed that it will be cooperative and we will need to see through their eyes as well as the children's eyes what happens and it's just a window in time and all that business and it will be cooperative until the point that it seems that the children are not first and foremost in everybody's mind. It's an equal opportunities issue.

Pamela sees it as a partnership but a limited one, 'My preferred model is one of the supportive role. Being in a partnership. Not necessarily Ofsted's model but mine and the contractors I tend to work for now are those that have that view.' She is able to:

> test out ideas and theories while you're in the school such as the issue of bullying. Parents may have raised a lot comments but you can't find the evidence so you share it and test it out with the school. It gives the school a chance to share with you what they haven't already dis-cussed at the interview and it will also throw up documents and evidence. It would be awful if you left it to the feedback and they said 'Ah, but we have this document and that document. If only you'd asked or we could have shown it to you.' So it's mutually beneficial.

Chris explains how this collaboration works:

> We get under the skin of the school by the Wednesday, I'm sure we do. More often than not the headteacher says 'Yes, that sounds just like my school, yes you've got under the skin of it, that's right. . . . You have created clear accurate analysis which tells us exactly where we're at, I agree with you, it confirms what I believed. It helps me know that I am going in the right direction'.

The respondent validation here seems conditional on agreement with the inspector. But others are more open. Simon, for example, likes to talk to the head about the findings:

> I think you can involve the school in it. You say, 'Look, this is what I'm looking at, this is how I'm looking at it.' You can involve them in part of the inspection process as well. I'd be quite happy to go with the headteacher into different things and say 'Look, this is what I'm finding in here, these are my judgments, this is what I'm basing it on, do you think I'm right or wrong, what do you think?'

Gathering an 'accurate' picture is hugely enjoyable as Pamela indicates. But she also admits to fallibility, and that she would take note of a school's response:

> I enjoy the fact that I can go into a school and find out a great deal about the school and come out with what I hope are accurate judgments. I feel it's successful if the school agrees that 'yes these are the same judgments we found' or 'I wasn't aware of this, yes that does need to be addressed.' I've not got it terribly wrong yet but it might happen.

Pamela tries to involve teachers in the inspectorial design, sharing their worries with them before the inspection, sending out a list of possible questions a head teacher and coordinators might be asked. However, the inspectors are in a contradictory position for operationalizing respondent validation, and they have widely contrasting experiences. On the one hand, respondent validation is reinforced by reciprocal relationships and events within the school. On the other, it is impeded by the inspectors' acute isolation.

There are many good moments which seem to cement relationships. For example, where there is good news for a school, it is an opportunity to celebrate the school's achievements:

> It's a good comment about us all if your school's done well. And for the LEA, that's good, another school's got a good report. Friends ring up and say 'Ah, that's good, got a good report on another school, great, can I come along and see that?' That's what you like to see.

There are many moments of delight for them as schools contact them to ask for more assistance, which they took as an endorsement of their judgments. A head nearing retirement who had a lot of new staff asked Neil if he would mind

> coming back for just half a day in September and just talk to them about what you did, what happened and say where we're going and say where you thought we were going wrong and then they'll tell you what they've done and we'll play it along.

In spite of their assertions that they don't offer advice at the same time as judgments, there is clearly some satisfaction in being looked upon as a valued interpreter, as Pamela discloses, 'There's the danger you might offer advice and you mustn't offer advice, but we all do it off the record you know — "you don't have to take notice of what I'm saying" but . . .'

However, there is another side to this excitement and pleasure of being freed from bureaucracy and the delight of becoming a respected specialist. At the same time as experiencing reinforcement through relationships, they experience the opposite effect — isolation — which can cause problems. Competition among teams bidding for an inspection exacerbates this situation. The independent RgIs find themselves not only isolated from colleagues in the LEA sector but from each other in terms of competing for quality inspectors. It's not only the problem of competition that isolates them, but fearful heads. 'The other dilemma is that whereas previously when an HMI walked into the school, I would guess the HMI had the confidence of the headteacher because of 150 years of HMI that went before. We have to earn schools' confidence.' They are not only isolated from some head teachers but also from many staff, as Pamela describes:

> It's the system that imparts this view of what an Ofsted inspector is and can be. You're perceived as the enemy. You're made very welcome when you come into schools. They're very polite and they're as helpful as they can be, but they don't want you there.

Her husband is a teacher in a secondary school:

> After their Ofsted party all the partners were invited but I wasn't. I'm an Ofsted inspector; I'm the enemy. You do notice silly little things in terms of the social world that you've got. You don't mention what you do because even old friends will change their reaction to you.

She also feels isolated from her previous work as a teacher and advisor. 'What I miss most is not having constant contact with the same groups of children. Doing inspections you don't really get to know them. You come across characters; they can be great fun but you don't really get to know them and see how they're getting on. We're all in it because we've got to earn a living as well.'

The media exposure and constant criticism of Ofsted is not helpful either. Neil feels HMCI

> lets us all down dreadfully on television and radio; I find it most offensive, and I do tell him. What's really sad is that the press are so bad at representing the inspection process. I can't imagine that our little company is unique, but to have one or two bad schools in total out of all the ones that we have done in three years is hardly a crisis situation. . . . (He) needs to say, 'out of 873 inspections, there are 17

that have been a real problem', which actually means that 98 per cent of schools are very happy with the process.

Nathan felt tarnished by a television programme about a secondary school inspection, which showed a teacher in tears, and two inspectors silently waiting until she had composed herself before going on with their report as if nothing had happened (B.B.C., 1995). Nathan thought 'the whole thing was done in a very vicious way . . . and yes, it did make me stop and take stock'.

Empathy
The inspectors tried to counteract their isolation by cultivating empathy — another well-known aid to validity in qualitative research. Inspectors are not oblivious to the kind of problems recounted in later chapters. They recognize the stress of the situation. Nathan

> was a teacher; I enjoyed teaching; I know it's a hard job; I've had HMIs in my room; some of them smiled at me; others didn't. I know that it can be draining and you do get involved in it; you do want the schools to do their best; you are pleased when you see something positive. You want to go away making the schools feel that they got something positive out of the experience. I understand the emotional drain which the inspectors have on them.

Pamela was made to realize the extent of how stressful the event is for teachers from her teacher husband's experiences:

> He'd got 20 odd years' experience. From my view he had no need to be concerned, but he was in school nearly every day of that holiday tarting the school up, checking everything was in place, that every-thing was ready. And I know damn well that all the other teachers are doing the same in their holidays and breaks. Headteachers tell me we have the school open at the weekends so that they can come in on Sunday and Saturday. They've probably been in there painting as well. It's ridiculous.

Pamela doesn't enjoy seeing teachers during inspection week:

> very anxious, tearful, sick, upset, worried that they haven't said the right things. . . . Telling you the next morning they didn't sleep all night because they've had an interview and they forgot to mention this, or they said this, or they should have said something else. . . . And also the anxiety that you get from heads. Some are very defensive, some quite antagonistic. Governors sometimes too.

Neil attempts to provide some cushioning:

If I give a 1 or a 2 or a 6 or a 7, we then go to the teachers after school, catch them and say, 'Hello, just a minute, I've just got to talk to you about this.' Before we do this, I tell the head that it's going to happen because if it was to happen to me I would want someone to pick me up, to look after me as a human being.

Whilst supporting the Ofsted aims, Pamela recognizes the long term effects on teachers of current changes:

I think it does provide rigour. It does improve the quality of provision and I think in the long term it will raise standards. But they've had a tremendous amount to take on and there's no stability in education which teachers can feel. The system keeps changing all the time. Change is good and it's useful but too much change and too little financial support and too little time support is damaging. They're being asked to work all the time.

She tries to be 'approachable' and 'reassuring'. She sets up 'communications with the headteacher at the start and end of the day so that if there are questions, confusions, concerns, we're aware of them'. They make allowances for special circumstances. For example, in one case where a teacher who had only been in the school one week was having difficulties

We tried to ease back a bit from her being inspected. We still have to inspect because we have to ensure coverage. But there are ways of talking to the headteacher and saying, 'Look, can we have a word to say that she needs to be a little bit kinder, softer with the children.' . . . Things like that can happen. You've got to show that you are sensitive to what they are feeling, to what they are undergoing as well still having to make the judgments. I've had another one in the middle of a lesson. Someone from admin. came in to say, 'Your husband's just phoned. Your son's had a very bad accident' and the first thing the teacher says is 'Oh, I must do that, I must do this' and I said, 'Just go, I'll sort it out with the headteacher.' Things like that. Someone else came in and said that their son had just been knocked over on a bicycle that morning, that they were in hospital and it turned out that they'd come into school because there was an inspection. It's nonsense.

Paul is aware of the effect of inspections on experienced as well as inexperienced teachers. Thus, when a fight broke out among pupils in a drama lesson with an inexperienced teacher, he was supportive, acting developmentally rather than judgmentally. The teacher

was in tears after it and didn't know how to handle it, and I felt it necessary to say that the challenge she had was enormous and that even the experienced teachers might not have handled it as well and that she should feel that her response to this totally unpredictable incidence was something which enhanced the profile of teaching in the school rather than reduced it. We're actually dealing with children who bring with them a whole load of emotions and anxieties and all the rest of it so it's not possible even for the most experienced teacher to predict events.

Triangulation

According to Fitz-Gibbon (1995), Ofsted's validity is compromised because of the difficulty of standardizing a great number of subjective judgments involved in observation. She has argued that the analysis of performance would be more effective if inspectors spent less time observing and more time analysing outputs. Observing is subjective and liable to variable interpretations as well as involving skills of being able to see through teacher performances which obscure the general reality of the classroom activity. Analysing, Fitz-Gibbon argues, would be more objective and focus more on achievement and progress. This argument is not accepted by the RgIs, however. They claim to be aware of any changed realities, and to use a kind of 'triangulation of methods' in coming to their conclusions. Simon, for example, claims to be able to 'see through performance if it's there because it just doesn't carry on somehow. You know when you look back at what they've done and how the class is organized and everything else that you can't change those things quickly, you can't put those on as a front'. Neil, also argues that the presence of the inspector doesn't affect the teacher a great deal, 'We sit with the children, we talk to the children, you don't even know I'm in there; I'm so small; I'm with the children. Now that sort of relationship of total involvement means that we have less impact on the teaching and we don't change their style. They usually change about the second day.'

They still want to sustain observation levels, therefore. In fact, Neil thinks there should be more,

> because it is the teaching that motivates interest etc. It keeps the children engaged with what actually leads to the outcomes, so it's very easy to spend a long time looking at work in isolation and not learn anything because of the way it's structured. The way it's recorded can also hide a lot of information, so I'd say they're (i.e. observation and analysis) parallel thrusts.

His argument is threefold, that Ofsted should be reporting on the quality of performance as well as performance outcomes, that these two are linked anyway and that outcome analysis may hide classroom realities. A mixed methods approach will, according to Neil, produce interesting insights and substantiate or challenge documentary evidence. Paul feels that, if inspectors are concentrating only on teaching, then they haven't got it balanced. It is possible to say at the end of the day that it seems that, in this group, children are learning in spite of the teaching or say, that the learning's not very good even though the teaching is very good.

Children in less privileged areas may be the ones who suffer most from an 'unbalanced' approach, the teaching appearing good, but not getting good results.

The inspectors also triangulate among the sample of personnel. Thus, Simon makes himself available to talk to other members of the community, so spreading his knowledge base of the school:

It might be that that evening they've got a special function on at 7.30 or 8.00, or the head says 'I've specially got some more parents to come and speak to you' and you make those judgments about them afterwards but you've got to take up that invitation. Otherwise you're seen as too separate and being too narrow and it's not good for the team.

They receive valuable input from the pupils:

It's talking with the children that you actually come to a view. You talk about work that's on a wall, what's it up there for. You say to a child, 'Which piece of work is yours, how did you do it, what did you do?' Say it's a painting, 'Well, what were the primary colours then?' You start asking them questions about it so you see if they understood the process, whether it was their work or not. I would say to a child, 'I want you to do a painting, would you be able to do that? What would you do?' If they say, 'We never get it out; we only have it once every 6 weeks or the teacher gets it out'; then you're in a position to say something about the children being independent workers. Now those things are about progression; they're about consistency between teachers; they're about what the child can and can't do in a broad sense, not just counting to 10 but organizing resources and preparing themselves, and working with others.

Triangulation helps solve the problem of the authoritative 'snapshot'. Chris argues that the snapshot is not the final piece of evidence, but a basis for discussion:

We go in; we meet the parents; we meet the school; inspect the school; we give them an oral feedback first of all; you give them a full feedback; you give a feedback to the governors; you increasingly give the feedback to parents as well. So it's not quite hit and we run. We have quite an increasing dialogue of feedback with the management team. Those subjective judgments are validated by spot notes and in terms of poor grading I go to the same lesson either with other inspectors, before them or after them, I have to check the grading and make sure we're seeing the same thing. And you're doing it together as well; you're spreading the work; you're saying, 'Here, look at this, what about this, what do you think of this?' So it's much more corporate I suppose, that part of it, doing it together. 'What do you think about Mrs X?' 'Oh I don't know, well I think she's a . . . , no Mrs X is really a 2 teacher; she's really very good; no I think she's a good teacher,' and 'she's a good teacher because . . . and what about that, she's not doing that so well'.

Validity here is based on comparing observations with either set standards or with other inspectors. It relies largely on trust of the professional expert and/or the triangulation process. But again there are mixed, contradictory messages in the inspectors' accounts. On the one hand, there is acceptance of the Ofsted model, managerialist discourse and conventional criteria; and research procedures which throw heavy emphasis on their experience, expertise and intuition. On the other, there is recognition of deficiencies and their fallibility, and what needs to be done for more rigorous findings. There are even signs in this respect that they employ an aesthetic model, at some odds with the Handbook approach. They realize that there is more to evaluating a school than simply adding up test scores or applying quantitative templates in a systematic way. The task calls for more artistic qualities. Simon thought, 'You've got to feel for what the nursery is about. You're going to have confidence that you can capture it in that light.' Chris also talked in these terms. They must continue to hone their skills in representing a school's likeness:

I think we're getting increasingly confident in analysing the school and writing very clearly and painting a picture of the school, with increasing clarity. I'll be a grandmaster by the time I'm 70. Being able to write more clearly, to present a clearer report, that's always the aim.

In summary, the inspectors' model of validity drew from both managerialist and professional discourses:

Managerialist Discourse	**Professional Discourse**
• Standardization	• Flexibility
• Sameness	• Difference
• Outer reality	• Inner reality
• Distance	• Closeness
• Observation	• Analysis
• Personal criteria	• Universal criteria
• Neutrality claims	• Values recognition
• Technical	• Artistic

Conclusion

It will be seen that there are a number of contradictions in the inspectors' perspective. They speak of the merits of distancing, while espousing a degree of involvement, engagement and feedback. They pride themselves on their expertise, but admit to fallibility. They believe in the merits of hierarchy and marketism, while indulging in some collegiality and cooperation with head teachers and governors. They revel in their independence and freedom, while singing the praises of accountability. Their views on validity encompass a faith in their own subjectivity, justification for the snapshot approach, a recognition of the need for research rigour, and a more qualitative kind of 'understanding'. Some are glad to have escaped the control of LEAs, but have arguably come under the control of a more constraining agency in Ofsted. They operate a technical-rationalist model, but use some humanistic methods. They articulate a managerialist discourse, while at times showing signs of a more professional/collegial one. They give qualitative feedback outside the terms of reference of the Framework. Teacher is seen variously as object, subject and colleague. They champion both artistic representation of schools and technical evaluation.

Some of these contradictions are more easily accounted for than others. We have characterized the stress they experienced as the kind that attends most professional positions. They believe they have more independence, but it relies on acceptance of the government's reforms and policies, and the Ofsted Framework. They reason that some are not contradictions in their eyes. Thus while some might perceive inspectors as carrying out a surveillance role, they see it more as a matter of accountability, a key element in the new work order. Other apparent contradictions may reflect a difference between ends and means. Thus, collegiality may be a way of inducing a technology of the self that allows

> individuals to effect by their own means or with the help of others a certain number of operations on their own bodies and souls, thoughts, conduct, and way of being, so as to transform themselves in order to attain a state of happiness, purity, wisdom, perfection or immortality. (Foucault, 1988, p. 18)

All the humanistic elements may be strategical devices to secure their ends, rather than being signs of an incipient alternative discourse. On the other hand, such differences may not be at all unusual. As Maguire and Ball (1994, p. 11) note, 'Discourse is only ever partial, is only one stance among many variants.'

Apart from the contradictions within, there is a huge contrast between the inspectors' perceptions of inspections reported here, and teachers' perceptions reported in subsequent chapters. We have to note that we only have the RgIs' experiences here, and they may not reflect the general experience of all the inspectors on their teams. Also, they were talking to us about their collective experience, and not just the inspections of our research. It may also be that the schools' presentations of front were only too successful, the most damaging consequences of inspections being shielded from the RgIs' eyes.

Whatever the case, it might be fairly assumed that they brought their mixed approach to the inspections of our research. The existence of a range of contradictions, we argue, arises largely from the inspectors' position in the chain of control. They face two ways. On the one hand is the government's educational policy and its approach to development and change, as mediated by Ofsted. On the other is the inspectors' own connection with teacher practice through their experience, values and ideology and their wish to implement a humane inspectorial process. Their official role is basically contradictory to primary teachers' expectations of how educational values and change are to be negotiated, and with how an advisory service might engage with teachers in evaluating current practice, as we discuss in Chapter 2. This is the origin of the inspectors' ambivalence and some find themselves at different points on this spectrum. 'Actors are positioned and constructed differently within different discourses' (Maguire and Ball, 1994, p. 12) — a comment that has a measure of truth, but leaves out of account the activity of the agents in defining their own position. Inspectors are not robotic agents simply systematically carrying out policies set out by others. They interpret their roles and their tasks, adapt some of their selves to the role, and some of the role to their selves. In this they are aided by a similar kind of latitude that teachers have hitherto enjoyed in applying the government's reforms. The 'implementation gap' — the degree of room for manoeuvre that customarily exists between policy making and policy implementation (Ball and Bowe, 1992; Fitz, Halpin and Power, 1994) — or the 'space of freedom' (Foucault, 1988, p. 153) allows inspectors room to develop their own particular discourse which encompasses elements of both contradictory positions. It is neither stark technicist, marketing, managerialism, nor is it humanistic, child-centred progressivism and democratic participation. There are bits of each in their views.

The inspectors in some respects appear to be trying to operate a kind of 'new' or 'humanistic managerialism' (Newman and Clark, 1994), seeking in their own practices to exploit areas of negotiative space to make human and professional contact with teachers. A complicating feature is that the whole Ofsted inspection process is about change as well as about assessment, and RgIs are caught with being both change agents and school evaluators. Their role involves assessment and control on the one hand, and change and development on the other. The two are in tension. Thus, although inspectors are being exhorted to talk to teachers more and engage with them more intimately, as many of the RgIs themselves would clearly wish, while the managerialist structure lasts in its current form, their basic relationship with teachers is likely to remain a supervisory one, albeit veiled in humanistic clothes.

Notes from the Field (2)
Monday — Early Encounters

After everyone had gone to their classes I found myself sitting alone in the staffroom. I wandered around a little reading the messages of good luck from parents, friends and one from the local inspector scribbled on a rough piece of paper by the secretary. I could hear the children coming into their classes but after a few minutes everything quietened down. I moved between chairs trying to decide where I would be relatively inconspicuous, as people returned from their classes at breaktime with news and stories. Once settled in a corner I began indexing some tapes of earlier conversations with some of the teachers. I was immersed in the drama but at a distance from the action.

At 10.20 the head popped in to say that the RgI had already made some complimentary comments to her about some of the lesson plans. She seemed pleased and relieved. She buzzed around tweaking a bit of organization here and there, reporting all positive comments and events and rushing off in mid sentence to do something else. This was not the General evaluating the battle plan and devising new strategies, she was ensuring that everything went smoothly, clearing away newly emerged obstacles, making sure papers and people were in the right place for the inspectors, reporting positive events and generally boosting morale 'I feel that the school will do well.'

At the first of the breaks in the action there were loud stories told of teachers' encounters, 'every time the door went I twitched' and told with humour, 'my first lesson was PE for three quarters of an hour. I leapt around very energetically. I hope they realize how much I had to fork out for the sports bra.' Another PE story shows their commitment, 'I did it in two left shoes of different sizes because I couldn't find a pair, and I was in agony the whole lesson, not that I let them see that.' When encounters went badly irony was used. 'One child hit another and I let a queue form — normal day really!' Terse descriptions capture the nature of the encounters. 'Why does it seem like there's more than four of them. They must clone each other. I've had hardly a moment without them.' Wounds are described, 'One of them asked the children what flowers they were painting and although I'd told the children a few minutes ago none of them remembered', and alleviation of tension sought, 'How I wished I smoked.' Other ways of coping are explored, 'I've put on my track suit. Do you like it?' asked one teacher modelling herself.

Laura is keen to assure me that she was confident about the event by telling me that she had been away for the weekend, slept well and did her preparation in school at 7.30 this morning. Others appear on a high but claim they 'can't keep this (level of performance) up for long. Shall we all have to play this role for ever.' Some return grateful to have survived and grateful for commendation, 'It was quite positive. He told me I had good control and the children were good at changing for PE. I was dreading it. I got confused at the start and mumbled my words. He said "thank you" and I said "thank you for coming". I was glad he said that I controlled them well.'

Another teacher recounts a close encounter, 'She sidled up to me and said quietly "I've never seen a file so neatly prepared." I touched her arm and said "thank you".' They played their part, 'In assembly two children were mucking about, my face glared and my voice said nicely "now come on".' The head-teacher asks the staff whether her assembly had gone OK and in the same breath she rushes off to sort out a loo roll stuffed down a toilet. The atmosphere in the school is, according to Linda, 'quiet and eerie. I can sense it is not normal. I can't here a sound at this end of the school.' She found the waiting intolerable. 'I just want them to come in and get it going.'

Halfway through the lunch break at 12.45, it is unusually quiet in the staffroom with even the loudest and most cheerful of staff lost in their own thoughts. Five minutes later there is a quiet hum as people talk quietly in twos and threes in a staffroom where the only accommodation is round the central table. Aileen gives Edith advice, Tracy and Letica discuss their practice, Elaine, Evelyn and Esther chatter quietly about non school issues, Laura works and Lional slides in and then leaves without a word. Five minutes on and Angelina arrives and the group all talk together for a while. Another five minutes later only four remain talking about home and life far from this event.

During the afternoon action the headteacher returns to the staff room to report that the RgI had said she was 'efficient' and it had pleased her because she wanted it to be like that for the staff and again as I talked to her she interrupted and rushed to the phone to tell her secretary not to buzz her room as the inspectors were conducting interviews therein. 'There's so much whirling round in my head. I've fished out two loo rolls from toilets today. The holders haven't been fixed. I don't want the inspectors to get there first. "Oh Marion (the secretary), I don't want to panic people but the stock room keys seem to be missing and matches have been seen down one of the loos".' She analyses her role, 'I'm acting like the Gestapo, checking up on smoking which we had here some time ago.' She leaves in a rush and returns half an hour later for some deodorant spray. 'I found some excrement over a loo door and I've cleaned it up.'

During the afternoon break one teacher bemoans that she has had no-one visit her whereas others have been visited constantly and another leaps into the room calling out 'A plus' in a loud excited voice. Another describes them watching some of his boring lessons in the morning and missing his good topic lesson that afternoon. 'If the science inspector doesn't come in by

Thursday I'll ask him in because I want him to see me. The science was good but he probably didn't come because I had written "topic".' Another exudes over her 'great kaleidoscope lesson' that was not seen by anyone. Nobody can determine where the action will take place. They're on their toes the whole time. The school support staff are both participants in the event and observers of it. 'The school is so calm, even wet playtime was different, the head helped out. I wish it was like this every day.'

The end of the first day in the staff room begins with a visit from a past colleague who arrives with three cakes. These are cut up and eaten amongst lots of chat about the day's events. In the middle of this the head apologizes and asks if they can all provide one below average reader for tomorrow. Elaine says the inspectors seemed impressed and were complimentary. Aileen looks pale and doesn't joke or laugh as she normally does. Emily tells her tale of a bruising engagement, 'she said that she couldn't find my drama lesson on my English termly plan. I chased after her and told her it was in my music/drama plans. She didn't say a word to me about my drama lesson. There was no feedback. I'm worried.' (She was right to be as things turned out). Letica tries to interpret inspectors' actions 'she talked to the children a lot. I emphasised place value, was that right? She's very thorough and she asked a lot of questions.' The stories subside as they turn back to the event's demands. Esther asks Laura to help her with her PE plans. It's decided that the new netball posts caused some arguments in the playground so they're being removed for the rest of the week. By 4.30 they are all back in their classrooms preparing for the next day though there is some solace in that the event is at least happening, 'I'm glad it's here. It's been a lot of hours out of my life.'

I left them alone the next day until after school had finished when I returned to hear the stories of the day.

Chapter 2

A Conflict of Values: The Teachers' Perspective

The government do not admit to being motivated themselves by any particular ideologies or discourses. To them it is the teachers who have suffered from ideology, for they have been under the influence of Plowdenesque child-centredness, which too often has left children to their own devices, been too woolly minded, neglected the basics, and been complacent about unsatisfactory standards (Woods and Wenham, 1995). The government's firm standpoint, on the other hand, represents a drive for 'common sense', straight thinking, and new forms of rigour (Ibid.). In effect, however, as we saw in the Introduction, the government — and Ofsted — are driven by a highly distinctive set of values, which are markedly opposed to those of a majority of primary teachers.

Ostensibly an independent body, Ofsted nonetheless operates within the boundaries of the policy reforms outlined in the Introduction. Some of those values are enshrined within the Ofsted 'Handbook', which contains the 'Framework' giving advice on inspection requirements; and guidance on the collection of evidence and the inspection process. The language of the 'Framework' is a technical one based in the concepts of audit and managerialism. Measurable factors predominate as they affect such matters as attainment, progress, strengths and weaknesses, effective and ineffective teaching, needs, management, resources, objectives, assessment, use time, competence, planning, skill. The model of the teacher and the learning situation provided in the handbook is essentially a transmissional one in which information is passed to pupils, and pupils are seen as developing through the manifest technical skills of the teacher. Phrases like 'contribution to pupil's attainment and progress', 'overall strengths and weaknesses in different subjects' 'effective teaching', 'the extent to which teaching promotes learning', 'secure knowledge and understanding of subjects', 'employs methods and organizational strategies which match curricular objectives', 'needs of pupils', 'manages pupils well', 'achieves high standards of discipline', 'assesses pupil's work thoroughly', 'uses assessments to inform teaching', 'uses homework effectively to reinforce and or extend what is learnt at school' illustrate the model that Ofsted prefers.

In this model, the child is seen as a pupil (rather than 'child'), *in need* of managing and disciplining and *needing* to learn certain prescribed things in order to be able to survive in a competitive market. The teacher is seen as someone who has to *impart* knowledge and understanding of a set curriculum, who *supplements* deficiencies, *assesses* and *evaluates* pupils' efforts from an hierarchical position, rather than one who removes obstacles to learning and works *with* children.

In terms of the inspection process, the language of scrutiny, evaluate, paying particular attention, judgments, observing, assessment, discussion, of forms, handbooks, schemes, policies, classrooms and other areas predominates. Pupil inspection, inspector observations and paper scrutinization are the means used to collect evidence on which judgments are based and recorded on Ofsted forms which contribute to the Record of Evidence upon which the final assessment of the school is constructed. Pupils and teachers are differentiated in this form of evidence gathering. Pupils are seen as customers or clients and teachers as service providers. The pupils and the teachers were not brought together to discuss mismatches, misunderstandings or misinterpretations. Instead the pupils were used to test the teacher's competence and the school's efficiency against a predetermined set of criteria. Provision or delivery again implies a transmission approach to teaching and learning and the existence of a body of knowledge that is the teachers' responsibility to impart. The separation of pupil from teacher, of pupil from person, of both pupils and teachers from their own knowledge (for their knowledge is downgraded in favour of National Curriculum knowledge and inspector knowledge) is in direct opposition to much of a primary teacher's practice.

Primary teachers' values since the 1960s are well known. In broad terms, they believe in holistic, integrated knowledge, child-centred teaching methods, a measure of professional autonomy, continuous and formative assessment, and collaborative teacher cultures (Nias, et al., 1989; Acker, 1990; Bonnett, 1994; Alexander, 1992; Vulliamy and Webb, 1993 and Sugrue, 1997). Most of the teachers in our six schools subscribe to these values. Unsurprisingly, therefore, there was a considerable clash of values between teachers and inspectors. We argue that much of the conflict experienced by teachers during the period of the inspections in their schools can be traced back to these basic values. In the rest of this chapter, we consider the teachers' experiences of the inspections at the level of values in relation to knowledge, pedagogy, assessment and culture.

Knowledge

The inspectors' approach appeared to teachers to be partial, focused on immediacy, unidimensional, compartmentalized and, standardized in contrast to teachers' own sense of holism, flux and complexity.

Partial

Robina (Flately), discussing a demand for a timetable based on subject teaching, said, 'It's a nonsense. I've done it for them and I'm going to be breaking my backside to constrain myself and say, "this is science, this is maths", because that's what they want to see . . . It's not really compartmentalized like that.' Inspectors drifted in and out of lessons, missing an introduction or leaving just as the activity started. They often didn't stay to hear the winding up of the lesson, much to the chagrin of the teachers who felt as if they were being treated as functionaries. Frank (Cottingly) found it

> an incredible attitude (and) bad manners. If you want to see what's gone on before, what the children contributed to the lesson, and what's going to happen, you'd rather have them in at the beginning of the lesson rather than just wandering in at anytime.

The inspector that interviewed Rosa (Mixstead) hadn't read her policy and other paperwork before he talked to her. He just gave her a list of questions 30 minutes prior to the interview and typed the answers into a laptop computer very slowly. There was no conversation, and Rosa was worried about 'going too fast'.

Kieran, at Mixstead

> saw the way that they came in and looked at three kids working on shape and that made four or five lines in the report and that is completely untypical of what's going on. I had the lady come in the middle of a Maths session, she browses around looking at different kid's work, pretends for 15 minutes, then walks out without speaking to me or anything. I think 'well, if that report is based on what happened in my classroom, I am afraid that is a joke . . . whether the comment is good or bad.

Immediacy

Aileen (Lowstate) recalled how one child in her pre-Ofsted inspection

> couldn't remember the name of the Dienes maths apparatus when asked and you feel as though that's just unfair to be judged on what a young child says. Although I had prepared lots of extension sheets, the children didn't realize that as they finished they could go on to B and C, but there was this instant judgment. Also they don't recognize the feelings and the encouragement that you've developed in the classroom. They're suddenly into their control. They're in control — when they walk in that door, we lose the children. They're in control of us and our perceptions of ourselves actually.

Letica, at the same school, reported a pre-Ofsted inspector's visit, and indicated where she thought the emphasis should be,

After 10 minutes observation I was deemed 'satisfactory'. If that means children who have been in school, just over half a term — and who are pretty well on the road to reading, is just 'satisfactory' I would dispute that. It was more than 'satisfactory' it was 'commendable'.

She was concerned that too much time was spent examining the teacher and not enough time was spent on the progress the children were making. To the teachers, inspectors often appeared unaware of the teacher's circumstances. One lead inspector interviewed a deputy head for most of the lunch time and as the bell went for the beginning of the afternoon, said 'I'll be up in a minute to see your English lesson.' The worst bit of Freda's (Cottingly) children's assembly was afterwards and

coming back in here and having about five minutes with the children and an inspector walking in to see the next lesson. It was like 'Oh, can you just leave me alone for a while', and I had to set them off on these mass investigations that they were doing. All the children were on a high, you know what assembly's like anyway. All their parents are there and they're all excited and suddenly it's all over as well, and it was just awful. I could really have just done with someone just leaving me alone for just 15 or 20 minutes when you just say to the class 'well done'.

Esther (Lowstate) found the strict timetable demands unsuited to teaching:

I was in the middle of a maths lesson which I would have continued except the bloody woman came in and said, 'Oh I just wanted to check, you are doing music at half eleven', and I thought, 'Oh sod it, so I had to stop the maths and do the music. We were following the timetable rigidly which you cannot do in the classroom anyway. Sometimes they've finished in two minutes instead of 20; sometimes they've finished in an hour instead of 10 minutes and it's just the way it works out.

The existence of different conceptions of teaching and learning were under-pinned by the assumption that teachers could be judged with such limited observation: 'They breeze in and breeze out and then make a judgment in four days on your whole career.'

Nancy (Morghouse) did not feel treated

as a professional worker who's been working at it a long time, you should be given some credibility for having some sort of intuitive know-ledge and instinct about things and you're not.

Unidimensionality

Inspectors did not discriminate between behaviours of what teachers saw as significantly different importance. The quality of progression in a particular subject was given the same status in terms of criticism as the fact that, 'not all the children could see the blackboard'. Linda (Lowstate) gave the example of a local inspector on a pre-Ofsted inspection who

> nit-picked over various things which I think we could justify the way we do things. He sort of warned us that this was what he was going to do so not to take it personally. Of course you're going to. He picked out things which to me were only a very, very small part of the whole but you were left with the feeling that 'oh that's it, we're judged on that'.

Erika (Mixstead)

> was just waiting for them to ask me, to talk to me about it, and I didn't get one single person talking to me, and I had everything ready for them, and they just didn't . . .

Thus they had no sense of progression from one lesson to the next, or what her aims were,

> yet they come in and say 'this worked, this didn't work' or whatever, 'she was doing this, wasn't doing that'. . . . I didn't want a discussion, but for someone to ask me what I was doing, why I was doing it!

Kirsty, at the same school, also had files, lesson plans and assessments ignored, and 'was never asked anything about anything'. She took the initiative in approaching inspectors, because 'I wanted them to have rapport with me so I could clarify or explain what was going on, or to get them to react to what they might say as a feedback to me.'

Primary teachers conceived of knowledge as being less concrete than the conception used by Ofsted:

> Even after 24 years in a primary school I just wouldn't dream of telling people I know everything. There are still different ways, I'm still making mistakes; there are still ways of approaching things that probably I haven't tried or should try or have tried and they've failed. (Veronica — Trafflon)

Teachers felt that the multiple goals of their work (A. Hargreaves, 1994) were not appreciated by Ofsted inspectors in spite of inspection categories, such as school ethos, that appeared to take into account social aspects of education:

> We're not saying that the education system didn't need a review because I'm sure it did, but it has meant that children have become slots in a machine who have to come up with the right numbers and we're the ones that have got to make them come up with the right numbers

whereas before you were dealing with the whole child. You were dealing with its emotions; you were dealing with its social life; you were dealing with its grandma; you were dealing with its physical development in a much more intense and bonding relationship than you do today. You had a real effect on these people and you felt that you were actually doing something that was worthwhile and they come back and see you and you're still 'Miss', you're still important to them. I was referred to as 'Miss' by a 29-year-old. Being that important to other human beings is a real privilege, but that joy has been dampened and dampened until I don't think it's a privilege any more. (Cloe — Trafflon)

Teachers therefore felt that inspectors failed to appreciate the integrated multidimensionality and complexity of their work. This may have had something to do with inadequate inspectoral methods, but there are indications that they were underwritten by different understandings of what work constituted.

Complexity

A headteacher elsewhere has commented:

It's a bit like an MoT (Ministry of Transport) test on a car. It tells you the state of the vehicle today, but can't take any account of the fact that it was a complete wreck last week, and that you've got plans to make it even better the week after next. (O'Conner, 1997)

An Ofsted inspection has similarities with an MoT in other ways. The mechanic has a plan of the car and is generally able to apply the plan to all cars. The mechanic examines a set of components for functionality and evaluates it in terms of good or satisfactory working order, and failure. The mechanic marks certain components as failing and then leaves the car owner with the responsibility of bringing the component up to standard or to replace it. However a curriculum cannot be so compartmentalized argues Toni from Trafflon:

The curriculum to my mind cannot be 'delivered'. Notionally it can be delivered but in reality it can't. If somebody says to me: '36 hours to implement the RE curriculum, an hour a week', I suppose I can do it, but when you bring it down to reality, no I can't do it.

The reality of the teaching and learning context is changed. Just as a car has a number of unconnected components, so does the focus of an Ofsted inspection. However, there is very little that is unrelated in a primary school or classroom. Assemblies often relate to individual achievement and appropriate learning behaviours; the form of questioning in a classroom relates to the teacher's particular programme for each child; the depth of record keeping on each child relates to the child's particular needs and the atmospheres that are created relate to different teaching and learning situations (Woods and Jeffrey, 1996b):

> How dare they come in and judge on one PE lesson, one science lesson, one this, one that — almost like going into Woolworths and, you know, Pic and Mix and have you got a full kilo at the end of it? (Cloe — Trafflon)

A car does not have feelings, aspirations or the capacity to make hundreds of qualitative judgments every day. Nor is it able to work morally in terms of justice, and other values. It is not in Aristotle's terms a 'virtuous being'. For teachers, it is this complexity — more representative of a living organism than a car — that Ofsted inspections are unable to grasp (Maw, 1995).

Pedagogy

The Chief Inspector has told teachers

> Our inspections have shown us which teaching methods work best and that knowledge ought to be disseminated as widely and quickly as it possibly can. I am a complete believer in the professionalism of teachers. It is not for the Chief Inspector of Schools to impose on you how you teach but it is my responsibility to ensure you have access to information about what is working. Children will learn more when teachers teach better. It is that simple. (Woodhead, 1997)

The Chief Inspector assumes that pedagogy is a neutral matter. Some methods, simply, work better than others. However, it might be argued that choice of teaching methods depends on a host of factors, such as one's objectives, view of knowledge, idea of the 'good society', interpretation of one's own pupils' needs, resources available . . . most of which are value impregnated. Opinions will therefore differ, at least to some extent, on what constitutes 'good teaching'. Also, while Woodhead might not exactly have been 'imposing teaching methods' on teachers in recent years, nobody has worked harder to secure an increase in whole-class teaching in primary schools. Ofsted, under the Chief Inspector's direction, have mounted a campaign for an increase in whole-class teaching, indeed, according to Woodhead (Hackett, 1995; Montgomery, 1996), it should constitute at least 60 per cent of a teacher's approach. It is the method best suited, arguably, to teaching a prescribed and controlled National Curriculum, and to prepare for the prescribed national assessment.

But while whole-class teaching is certainly used to some degree by our teachers, as one of a range of techniques available depending on purpose, it is not one, given this emphasis, which best suits our teachers' values and beliefs.

For their child-centred approaches, group and individual work have higher priority. Dora (Morghouse) felt that the Ofsted 'form' was expected of her as a teacher:

> 90 per cent of my teaching is done with small groups or individuals on a one to one basis or at the little board there. I do very little front of class teaching, while I am actually doing that, the others are organizing themselves to the tasks that I've set them. They do very well but you feel as if you should either be in front of house or there in the middle, this all-pervading presence.

Ironically, Corrine (Trafflon) supported the idea of inspections and saw the imparting of knowledge to her children as paramount but found herself restricted by the tight examination of her planning encouraged by Ofsted:

> I think, at the end of the day people will end up being less efficient, There's no opportunity to deviate from the plan if children need to tackle a prior skill in order to benefit from what you are teaching, it's constant teaching. . . . I was just functioning, I was not relating to the children, I wasn't teaching them. . . . I was doing testing from paper to the children, but I don't think they were learning. I was not making things clear to them. If a child didn't understand, I would have to say 'Sorry, it's too late, it's too bad, you have to listen because I have to go on to something else, I have to follow my plan.'

There are other points of difference. Primary teachers invest a great deal of their own selves in their work (Nias, 1989). They see their classroom work as extensions of themselves. The teacher role is a humanized one, both with regard to teacher self and to relationships with colleagues and children. They believe in cultivating trust. They place a high priority on feelings in teaching and learning, and on making emotional connections with knowledge and with children (Woods and Jeffrey, 1996b). Veronica (Trafflon), for example, believes that fun is a powerful tool to gain enthusiasm. She used to play games with her children but

> I haven't had many laughs with this lot this year; it's disappearing fast. They might sound stupid or silly things but they get the kids' interest. I might just write something on a piece of paper and stick it in my pocket and the children say, 'Oh go on Miss, Oh go on, tell us what's on it' and I'll say 'If you're very good I might tell you tomorrow.' And they come bombing in the next day, 'What was on that piece of paper?' and I say, 'Are you sure you want to know? Well actually, it's about some difficult work we have to do next week which will in the long term help you.' I know that the week after next I'm going to attempt so and so and it's quite a difficult area and I want the children to be open minded and enthusiastic about it. How do you write all that on a plan? I can't do it.

By contrast, Ofsted inspectors appear to see things in rational, unemotional, almost dehumanized terms. According to the discourse of the 'New Right', there has been too much woolly, romanticized thinking in teaching, and not enough hardness in appraising facts and rigour in prosecuting tasks. One of the mantras of the time has been, 'There's been too much caring, and not enough teaching' (Woods and Jeffrey 1996b, p. 54). Ofsted inspections, therefore, are designed to cut through these emotional layers to the bare realities that lie at the heart of effective teaching, and then to bring these to prominence and build on them. Unsurprisingly, therefore, there was conflict in this area.

Erica (Mixstead) was a prime example of this investment of self. She was a first year teacher, aged 26, who had worked in a financial institution and was experiencing her Ofsted inspection after six weeks of teaching:

> I feel really comfortable with this group. I can really be myself . . . I really feel at home. . . . When I am sat here with the children, and we are talking, whether it be informally or teaching, it is me as a person in there as well teaching . . . They seem to respond well to you if you are a person as well (as a teacher), so it is a sort of mutual getting to know each other and working well together. Rather than be somebody who is really removed, I want them to be able to approach me.

Rita's (Mixstead) husband, who worked in commerce, saw employees as functionaries, and could list a number of teachers who, for what he knew of them socially, he would dismiss, but his wife argued that

> It isn't commerce . . . (and) these are people that I know come alive in the classroom and are completely different people, and what you have got to remember is that you're working with a number of little bodies, who have all got to get out of bed, hopefully on the right side and you have got to hit on the right formula because this child could have had a row with mum before he had come to school.

Teachers projected their humanity on to the inspection teams, who displayed a certain detached, authoritarian approach. Kirsty, from the same school, for example, saw them as

> human beings just like me, and they are probably just as worried doing an inspection as I am on the other side of the fence, so therefore why make them appear to be stony people trying to find faults with the systems? Why not try and nurture a better bond. When they walked past my open plan classroom in those two and a bit days I made a point of acknowledging them. Kayleigh, my job share, said to me that she had not one bit of a relationship with anybody. Now, I am a different person to her anyway, so I thought 'Right, that is not going to happen to me, I am going to make sure that I have a rapport.' With some of them I didn't; they were very unapproachable.

Rachael, her headteacher, also challenged the RgI's authority over what she considered to be unacceptable behaviour from one of the inspectors. He was reported to have been rude to two of her teachers:

> I wasn't demanding an apology. I was just stating a point, but he didn't like it. He was definitely colder on that day than he had been any other day. He was saying that it was a very difficult task for his team. I wouldn't take that. I said 'I have listened to what you said, and I still want to speak to the man directly.' That man had not even acknowledged my presence, never spoken to me at all, and I said 'I am sorry but I find it very hard to be in a position of responsibility myself and find that one person has totally ignored me.' They took over my school; it's no longer mine.

Erica compared the inspection with teaching practice, which was 'completely different. They were advising; they were there; they were talking to the children; they weren't just sat there with a straight face'. By contrast, during the inspection,

> I said 'Oh, would you like to have a seat?' I emphasized it. I wanted to make it clear that she could have my seat, but she didn't take it. She just said she had notes to write. She had my file in front of her with my lesson plan and group details in it, so I had to get up and crawl through the children to get the list off the wall. Even things like that throw you, when you haven't got a group list, because I normally have it in my file beside me. I couldn't have it because she was looking at it!

When the formal work she was doing did not go well because she detected her children were nervous in the presence of the inspector, she

> just stopped it all, and then got them on to the carpet and got them to read the story and did some show and talent work instead, because I wasn't happy with the way it was going. I just wanted to get rid of the inspectors; it wasn't going right.

She felt that she had lost control, and that

> it could have got beyond me. When I was in my other job I was put in complete control, and that's how I normally like to feel in the classroom. I just felt it was getting out of hand so I closed it down.

She felt under pressure from Ofsted to change her teaching style:

> You want to be maybe a bit safer (in the inspection week) than you might be. Whereas, sometimes you want to react to what the children

do but you have to have everything so laid out in advance. Like the electricity when the children wanted to know about switches. In my plan I wanted to do 'series' next. In the end I took the option we would look at switches that day because they had the enthusiasm then; they were asking questions about switches so I did it. But, I didn't know if it was the right thing for them, because really the next progression would have been to do series, looking at more than one bulb, but I didn't because I went with the children.

The spotlight that was used to focus on the detail of a teacher's work diminished the opportunity to be examined in terms of one's values and beliefs,

> I never get the chance to think of my philosophy any more, my beliefs. I know what I believe but I never really put them into words any more. Isn't your philosophy more important than how many people get their sums right? (Bronwyn — Cottingly)

Clare (Trafflon) supports this approach:

> It's not changing my teaching one iota apart from Ofsted week. I can't change my teaching because my teaching comes from inside of me. I'm one of the old types of teachers born to be a teacher . . . I have a feeling for children and their needs.

Teachers' relationships with children were scrutinized in terms of the quality of teaching and learning, their classroom control, organization, and their performance was evaluated on a seven point scale. They were quizzed as to the organization of their curriculum responsibility in terms of how they measured achievement and how they monitored other teachers, and they were quizzed about the general organization of the school to provide evidence of implementation of published policies. Teachers were not usually spoken to by the inspectors except when they were being questioned, though some inspectors did make a comment about a lesson from time to time.

Assessment

The major issue here revolved around inspection as monitoring, policing, secretive, checking, archiving and using quantitative measures, against inspection as developmental, involving advice and feedback, formative, open, based on discussion and the use of qualitative methods. Teachers' experiences of Ofsted inspections were overwhelmingly of the former kind. Their experiences equate with the view of Ofsted inspections as the cutting edge of the government's reforms in a Foucaultian moral technology. Ball's analysis (1990b) of appraisal in the 1980s applies *a fortiori* to Ofsted inspections in the 1990s:

Appraisal has become one of the prime features of the political reconstruction and disciplining of teachers as ethical subjects in the 1980s. It
extends the logics of quality control and performance indicators into
the pedagogical heart of teaching. It brings the tutelary gaze to bear,
making the teacher calculable, describable, and comparable. It opens
individuals to an evaluating eye and to disciplinary power. (p. 159)

Feedback

From the teachers' developmental, professional point of view, it seemed natural
that inspectors should offer advice and give feedback. But inspectors were not
generally involved in that kind of exercise. Teachers were there to be 'known
and recorded' by inspectors in a 'formal ritual of power and ceremony of visibility, a technology of objectification' (Ball, 1990b, p. 159). This necessitated
distanced, hierarchical monitoring. Deena (Morghouse) found herself sitting
with a group of children with the lead inspector sitting behind her:

> I could just feel him there. I felt as though I was doing all the right
> things but it affects you mentally. That evening I suddenly thought,
> 'Oh I could have taken that child to do that.' If he hadn't been there
> maybe I could have been more natural. I wondered if he was sitting
> there thinking, 'Oh she could do so-and-so; she could take this.' I just
> wondered 'Why couldn't it be natural and why he couldn't suggest
> things, if he's the expert and he's got the good ideas or whatever, or
> he feels I'm not actually stretching those children enough, why can't
> he just tell me?' To think somebody has sat there and there were
> reams written on that sheet! . . . No matter what they say about the fact
> that they're looking at the children, it is a judgment on you and your
> classroom, and I want to know how I've been judged. Not for any
> other purpose other than that it's mine, that it is about me and I want
> to know it.

Kay (Mixstead) observed that:

> It was bad, because you were just under scrutiny, and you are not told
> right or wrong. I didn't pull back the woman who came in when I was
> doing maths; she didn't see the presentations; she just saw them re-
> cording and I don't think that is a fair judgment. She never said a word
> to me; she didn't even look at me. All that I got was when one of the
> men came in and spoke to me, and they were very enthusiastic saying
> 'this is good, this is good', but it's not real feedback, it's empty words
> because you don't see what they are actually writing. He wrote down
> a lot more than 'this is a good lesson'.

Lack of this kind of interaction diminished the teachers' sense of identity. Kay did manage to have a chat with her RgI. Without it, she

> would not know where I was in that I would wonder 'Is that me they are referring to? Was it me here? Was it me there?'. . . . I am in the unusual position of having had a direct report, which other people didn't have.

Even when there was some feedback, it was felt that it was often banal and obvious,

> I think it looked like a fairly crappy science lesson, because they were basically doing a worksheet but it was the follow-up of all the other work that we had been doing about growing up. I was able to go to him and say, 'we're doing this because we're following up this and this and I showed him those books we'd made and he came back the next day and said, 'Oh it was a really interesting way that you were doing that' and he talked about it. I thought, 'Well it wasn't a new idea or anything; it was the way you would do it with Infants; does he not know that?' (Esther — Lowstate)

The final feedback — the report — didn't satisfy Dora (Morghouse) on two counts:

> We knew as professionals before they even started the sort of things they were going to say — the buzz words that are going round at the moment, 'monitoring', 'learning', 'recording' — more paperwork in other words. We have had a very positive feedback in the report but it's all very bland. 'You're very good; you're very expert; the children are a credit to you. But let's have a bit more on paper'. It just brings you down.

Surveillance

Teachers felt they were under surveillance. They were not just being observed in a constructively critical way in an enterprise in which they and inspectors had shared aims. Our dictionary defines 'surveillance' as 'close observation or supervision over a person, group etc., especially one in custody or under suspicion'. There was a supervisory edge to the inspectors' observation, and a pronounced flavour of 'suspicion'.

A first year teacher at Flateley felt

> more confident when I was on my teaching practice than I was here in this inspection. It was this idea that 'Oh, she's gonna really find out

that I can't teach!' I'm supposed to be a professional . . . a fully fledged teacher and I think now that security, of being a student, who was allowed to fail in some areas was taken away. I felt more harassed or more aware of this woman because she was more of an official body, in my eyes, watching me . . . When I was in the nursing profession, we were continually being assessed, but nothing to this scale and they were people who've got other peoples' lives in their hands but they never had this sort of assessment, this 'big brother' watching you. (Simca — Flately)

Their distance makes the experience meaningless:

If you are talking to a particular child and they suddenly start writing a lot, you think 'Is that right, have I done it right? Perhaps I said the wrong thing?' So I don't think it is much benefit at all. It just put everybody on edge, you could cut the atmosphere with a knife half the time. (Kay — Mixstead)

Ofsted keep their evidence, and details of how it was come by, to themselves. They

just came in and wrote, wrote, wrote, looked, looked, looked, got up and walked out again and to my dying day I will never know what they thought about me . . . I really do resent it. They're like doctors' notes in that you don't know what they've written about you. It's kept private from you and not shared with you, plus what the hell is the point of it all if you're not going to get any better? . . . I think it's just the secrecy of it, the idea of this being written down and filed about me without being told what it is. (Esther — Lowstate)

The surveillance involves hidden process but public outcomes. They proclaim the results of their inspection to the world.

Archiving

As part of the 'examination', an extensive and 'meticulous archive' is constructed. School policies and programmes, teacher achievements, plans and progress etc. are carefully prepared and stored on file. Decisions about performances, weaknesses etc. are committed to writing, 'making it possible to classify, to form categories, to determine averages, to fix norms' (Foucault, 1979, p. 178). This is not the way that some primary teachers are wont to work:

I'd always throw myself into things to prove that I was of value and that's actually not enough anymore. I'm not particularly intellectual in my thinking, I'm more a doer than a thinker but you've got to lock into these bloody terminologies now or you've had it, haven't you; you've got to think certain ways and that's quite hard. (Carol — Trafflon)

Consequently, they felt constrained to develop what many of them considered inappropriate planning and record systems. Otterley (Mixstead) found the paper-work getting in the way of her teaching:

> While you could be interactive with a child and actually develop their language, you are finding that you are having to write an observation, so whereas 20 years ago, it was no writing and lots and lots of language which I love, now if you observe it you write it down, the next steps, and then you do an activity to continue. It makes you very aware of the individual child, that is the excellent thing. . . . But have you seen the record that we have to do now? 14 pages for every child.

The creation of paperwork allowed it to become something that could be examined, and at the same time introduced the idea that constant monitoring is possible via paperwork. The plans had to contain such things as content, methods, outcomes, differentiation and evaluation. When one head teacher (Dan — Morghouse) employed a team of inspectors from outside the borough to give the school a pre-inspection test, they asked him after three days invest-igation, 'How do you know what your teachers are doing?' He replied that he walked around the school a lot, taught regularly, that the teachers constructed the school's policies, that he saw their termly plans, that he knew his teachers, and that they all worked in a climate of professionality. The inspection team argued that this was not enough, and that he needed weekly and daily plans from them so he could check that they were doing the right thing in the correct way. Veronica observed that the demand for detailed and extensive records 'has left me with an even greater feeling of inadequacy than I had before . . . there's no trust that I am doing the job to the best of my ability and that I'm trying to cover all the curriculum during the year'. Teachers are 'hav-ing to write down the hidden things that you take for granted' and every component part is being examined. Naomi (Morghouse) felt that she had

> to chop the top of my head off and show somebody what's in it. 'Is it OK? You don't like what you see? Then I'll go and get another one.' For God's sake, they are just giving people more and more work to do because they have to check up on more and more people and they can't do their own job in the end . . . It's crazy.

For Shula (Flately) 'All my skills and expertise have been reduced to seven pieces of paper.' Rosa, who organized all the special needs at Mixstead, bought herself a photocopier for home because it means I don't have to stay after school photocopying. When I am here I want to be teaching. I have to make sure there are copies around because the inspectors will want copies of the IEPs (individual educational programmes). . . . It is about the unknown isn't it? It's about whether they will ask you for the piece of paper you haven't got and I've got over 200 in this file alone. You don't know whether they are going to say; 'Can I see the IEP reviews for the last year?' When I started writing them I didn't know we were going to have an inspection, so I now worry about whether they are in my best handwriting. Is the grammar correct? Have I made a spelling mistake? Does it all tie up? Will it be obvious that the ones that I have written this term are much neater and better than the ones that I wrote last term? It is all those things at 3 am in the morning. You have a vision of a headline in the newspaper 'Special needs that were written badly' and we've gone down the plug hole. And you imagine that all your friends you meet in the street are saying; 'Oh hello Rosa, I read that about the special needs. It is true isn't it? Isn't it awful?'

Measurement

The need for standardization, normalization and objectification required in-spectors to use, in the main, quantitative measurements. Thus, the culmination of the examination of individual teachers is a quantitative one with teachers being graded by the simple expedient of adding up the number of low graded lessons and judging a teacher as poor in the final analysis if they had more than 50 per cent of low graded lessons. This is marked contrast with the teachers' preferred qualitative assessment of their work.

Otterley (Mixstead) noted the difference with her Ofsted Early Years inspector:

She kept saying 'What do you want to have achieved by the end of the year?' I said 'every child developing to the maximum potential', but I think, from reflection, the answer she wanted was numbers to 10 or reading book one or six.

Her headteacher, Rachael, shows her distrust of ways of measuring that do not yield meaningful results:

What's going on, in the name of the education of children? Not what I want to see going on in primary education. I feel cross that we can't have any consistency at all and therefore we can't believe it. All they come up with are these stupid little tables. There are horrible things happening in education and in the name of getting a little test result out, but we are not in competition with the other schools here. I am attempting to provide a good education for the children who come here. I don't need to be in a league table. However, if there is a ball game to be played; you've got to play it haven't you? The press release about our inspection report relates to everybody here and that is why I've got to protect people.

Rita, her deputy, agreed:

I am around this school a lot of the time, and I see what goes on . . . but we don't go and sit in a classroom with a clipboard. I have had it done to me lots of times, and I don't like it . . . (perhaps) because they're not able to react fully to the classroom. I can monitor what goes on in a classroom without a clipboard, and I can interact with the children and yet come away and write a very full report.

Diane (Morghouse) argued that she should be part of the process:

They've reported that some science lessons were not as good as they could be . . . but I can also do self-assessment. I actually didn't need them to say that my lesson wasn't too great. The difference between the self-assessment and them making the assessment is that they write it down in black and white for everyone to see and secondly I can put mine right. I can then compare my next effort with my previous effort, but they've taken a snapshot of it. They won't be coming back to find out if the next time I do it any better, and even if it is they won't tell me.

Dora (Morghouse) was concerned about their professional qualifications:

It's a joke really isn't it? I feel that when you have somebody coming in to watch you teach there are two things they should be looking at or they should be aware of. Are you interesting to listen to; do you know your stuff, and are you presenting it in such a way that the child receiving it is going to get a lot from it and are you on the ball as far as knowing what's going on around you? I don't think that a secondary science teacher is the one to tell me if I'm OK or not.

Clare (Trafflon) thought that there was too much emphasis on SATs results and felt concerned for the consequences for the teachers as professionals:

We are probably going to have to change our practice because we know other schools were giving them extra help and extra time to finish. There was a complete disadvantage for our children because we didn't do that and it made our children look bad in the public eye. I haven't talked to our year 6 teacher but I would guess she'll be doing revision a hell of a lot earlier and that she will be a hell of a lot more forceful. It's cramming . . . for a test which has no purpose.

Cloe, in the same school, felt that the measurement of the children was crude and compromised her for selecting children for this process:

You've got to find out whether the school is coming up to scratch, but you don't fire questions at these six. It was as though these six children had big stars of David on them; it was a bit like the holocaust; it was, zoom in. This guy just comes straight in, 'What's 5 per cent of 250? Draw an equilateral triangle. Draw a right-angled triangle.' It's not in their experience to be treated like that also, I wouldn't have chosen those particular children. We were told to choose them for progress and I didn't choose them to see how well they could react with questions being fired at them. It was like 'so I'm going to see how good you are'. These people must have come out of the dinosaur age.

The quantitative assessment process was not used to benefit teachers. Edith (Lowstate) was doing long term supply at the time of the inspection and was criticized for losing control of some of her pupils in one lesson and for not having a good display but in talking it through a week or so later, it appeared that inspectors had made at least nine visits to her classroom:

The way they came up to me and spoke to me made me feel like I'd really let everyone down, made me feel that I hadn't done things correctly. However, if had been told that seven visits out of nine were satisfactory, I would have been walking with my head held high, given that I was a new teacher and being assessed for the first time. But I wasn't. I was only told that one of them was unsatisfactory. I was thinking of not coming back to teaching again. I like the staff here and I like the children so I'd like to stay but now with these people saying this about me, I wondered what the head was thinking. Was she thinking of keeping me?

Esther (Lowstate) found her inspection

a very negative experience, even after the nice bloke who watched the PE lesson was quite complimentary about it. He said, 'You've got some lively children in your class, haven't you, but you've got some pretty good strategies for dealing with them' At first I was quite pleased, and then later I thought: 'why on earth should I be pleased with him telling me that I know how to deal with some naughty children?' If I didn't know by now, I bloody well need shooting after 25 years! . . . I know whether I'm a good teacher or not — I don't need him to tell me.

Culture

It has been argued that teacher culture is undergoing profound change (D.H. Hargreaves, 1994). With respect to the schools of our research, Ofsted appear to be bringing influence to bear on teacher culture in two respects in particular: in formalizing relationships, and in promoting an atmosphere of blame, guilt and failure.

Relationships are at the centre of the primary teachers' working life. Amongst themselves, they value a strong, collegial, supportive culture (Nias et al., 1989). With the children, they seek to develop close, affective rapport. It is these ties with children that give their teaching meaning (Nias, 1989). The inspections transformed these relationships into more formal, functionary connections.

Breaking Attachments

Whilst unifying the school through a 'contrived collegiality' (A. Hargreaves, 1994), an Ofsted inspection breaks professional attachments. Reen (Mixstead) spoke of competition entering relationships:

> mainly because staff don't want to seem less than anybody else. I didn't want my display to be seen less than anybody else's, and so the fact that I have put in 40 hours was part of that and part of not wanting to let the side down, and part of wanting not to be criticized on any front.

Feelings about different work rates were exacerbated, Ava (Lowstate) feeling

> more strongly about a colleague who doesn't do anything and I do all the written work. That doesn't bother me because I quite enjoy writing things but then you begin to think: 'Why should she get the benefit of all these things I've written?'

Professional attachments were also broken through the intensification of teachers' work in the period leading up to Ofsted. It meant that older, more experienced teachers had less time to help new entrants to the profession:

> When you see someone who's been working in the profession for so many years, looking very harassed and worried, then that is, to me, quite daunting. If I had come into a school that wasn't being Ofsteded then those people would be able to support me a lot more than they're able to now. I imagine that they would be walking into my class and saying, 'How are you doing?', but they can't because the pressure is on them. They're probably looking at themselves being

inspected. So it is very much about people keeping themselves to themselves. (Simca — Flately)

Teachers did work hard to keep Ofsted's influence from dominating their time. Helen (Cottingly) noted that the subject of Ofsted was purposely kept off the staffroom agenda in an attempt to arrest its ever-increasing influence, but this left her frustrated:

> There are no discussions about feelings and the actions or the whole Ofsted thing in formal meetings. It might be assumed that we all know how each other feels and we probably do. We have all moaned, but I don't think anyone has actually sat down and discussed how we are going to cope that week, how are we going to approach it. However, if we do that and make a big thing out of it, it's going to make people think 'Oh, I haven't thought of that!' and worry people even more.

In this way, the innermost self is suppressed. There is no time for it to be brought into action. Isolation in schools is caused by people being too busy sorting themselves out, by staff not wishing to discuss Ofsted practices in their resting moments in order not to exaggerate the situation and make things worse, by staff meetings where the agendas are concerned with how to manage the technology of the inspection rather than the effects of the inspection, or, as in some schools like Flately, cancelling meetings to allow staff to work in their classrooms and thus isolating them further. In Aileen's (Lowstate) terms it makes you more 'self absorbed. I am perhaps over sensitive, concentrating on me, and maybe we're taking it too much on board and not looking at the grand plan of this. It's one of those professions where you can get terrible wrapped up in yourself and I think the Ofsted perpetuates that'.

The awarding of teacher grades against the wishes of most of the teachers further isolates teachers. As the implementation of teacher grading was only introduced during the research on the two last schools of the six we have only two examples of grades being given for excellent teaching, both in the same school. Two other teachers were commended quietly by inspectors in other schools but not given a grade and they were encouraged to keep this quiet from their colleagues, further isolating them. Where grades were given, one teacher felt it was due reward and the other was surprised, didn't particularly want the award and found that it affected her relationships with the other staff. Public discussion of their awards was muted for different reasons. Larry (Lowstate), who was commended, argued that individuals should take responsibility for their own performance (see Chapter 5) and that the awards could be more public but the secrecy surrounding the award and his membership of a corporate team meant that he felt it was necessary to keep quiet about his award. In the second case, Amy, in the same school, who was opposed to awards, became further isolated from the other staff. She recognized the variability of excellence — any teacher could be good on her day:

I haven't mentioned my grading at all. I don't think anyone would dare because I've been so aggressive about it. That's because it made me feel hugely uncomfortable. I'm one of the stronger teachers in the school and that's not being arrogant. But on lots of weeks there'll be lots of people who'll have a better week than me. . . . (Moreover) the number that has been stuck on the hat that I'm wearing is not my idea of respect.

The grading process separates and isolates teachers firstly because it differentiates between them in terms of competency, and secondly because the award of grade comes from the inspector rather than colleagues.

Key Stage 1 in Amy's school was criticized for the quality of teaching although the staff didn't accept the evaluation. A few weeks after the grade had been given, the headteacher decided to move Amy to Key Stage 1 in spite of her lack of experience in this department. 'She decided to put me in there, although I had only taught for 4 years, and had never been in a Key Stage 1, on the basis that I got an excellent grade. So how are those people going to feel, who have been doing it for 20 years? It's not going to enhance my position with my colleagues, is it?' Larry felt encouraged to make a professional connection with Amy based on the grading which would have further separated her from her colleagues. 'I still feel uncomfortable about it. I don't like talking about it. It's caused a lot of anger, upset, and I don't see any way it's made things better. I had an argument with Larry in my classroom because he came in and stopped the lesson and said "all right" like we were great buddies, we were in a club.'

Larry's feelings about his work were enhanced by the inspection (Woods et al., 1997), but he distanced himself from his friends and colleagues. Leila, one of his colleagues, shows how this happens:

Oh I couldn't bring myself to live with Larry . . . I couldn't face him. I couldn't bring myself to look at him or smile, I kept away. And we're quite friendly. Mm, I don't think he really is an excellent teacher. And I couldn't bear him being smug. I'll give him his due, he didn't mention it, but he kept grinning, that's why I wanted to punch him! I think the whole grading system is just a divisive thing to put teachers against teachers. You just feel that you're competing against each other and even with the best will in the world, you're going to get niggled if you know the person you're teaching alongside gets a better grade than you. If you've put in a lot of effort you must feel aggrieved. . . . It won't be confrontational but you're going to be churning up inside thinking 'that's not fair, he only got that inspector to come in because he knew he was going to have a good lesson'. I'm not that sort of person that does that.

Deena asked for some feedback on her work, but the RgI,

. . . said that he will only do it if everybody has it done, if everybody wants it whereas I wanted to do it quietly, keep it confidential. So everybody's going to have this feedback next Friday and I think that's another problem now because not everybody wants it. So that makes me feel bad because I feel a bit guilty about it because that's put more stress on other people, if somebody doesn't want it, why should they?

Teachers also found their relations with pupils, an essential part of their effective teaching, coming under threat. At the beginning of the term of his inspection, for example, Kieran felt he was being 'even more short tempered' than normally with his pupils in his efforts to 'set the right standards' — 'because if you don't get them right to start with then you always get the comebacks later on, especially when you feel that people are going to come in to see what you have been doing'. The inspectors themselves were considered detached from the children. A supply teacher at Mixstead who supported inspections felt they didn't communicate, they 'just walked round and when they did say something to the children they just asked them what they were doing, and went away'. Rita (Mixstead) described how she had encouraged her children to relate positively to adults:

They would approach somebody that is sitting in the corner and say, 'Look what I have done'. I had somebody who came to moderate my SATs and she was just sitting there with a piece of paper watching what was going on and a child in my class wanted to show her something that he had made, and it was, 'Not now' and he pushed him away and there were tears and everything, and to me that is not valuable at all, it is somebody jumping themselves up and I hope that is not going to happen. I like a lot of laughter. To me that is what makes a classroom tick, the odd aside from the laughter that goes on, the familiarity.

This detachment also applied to the inspector–teacher relationship. Teachers were encouraged not to speak to the inspectors, and the inspectors, in most circumstances, deliberately distanced themselves from the teachers — 'they never look you in the eye'. Rosa, a special needs teacher at Mixstead, observed their detachment from both teachers and children, as she moved around the school from class to class:

I know it is not about putting people at ease, but I think they failed dismally because they didn't put the kids at ease either because they weren't relaxed. They weren't particularly relaxed with the children and they didn't sit amongst them. I would've thought they would have involved themselves more with the children than they did. They were as tense as we were. They didn't speak to you in the corridor. I can't understand the fact that they don't acknowledge you even with a smile.

They didn't say 'good morning' or 'hello' or anything. It's very strange when they're here for so long. . . . They just set themselves apart.

The particular lesson for which Edith (Lowstate) was criticized was one where the visiting inspector sat directly opposite her at a distance of three to four metres when she was talking to the children on the carpet.

At first I thought, 'I'll just ignore them and do my own thing', but it's not easy if they are sitting right opposite you and writing, you're bound to deviate from the norm. You change, that was why I had a bit of a problem because she came right up and sat in front of me. When they come in they shouldn't make you feel tense, they should sit somewhere and just be watching not right in front of you.

This formalization of relationships is in direct opposition to the kind of culture that primary schools nurture, that of humanistic relations based on collaboration, collegiality, negotiation and sensitivity.

A Culture of Blame, Guilt and Failure

It's like having a surveyor round to look at your house. They are not going to come around and say; 'Oh, yes everything is fine, everything is great.' It's their job to find fault. (Katrina — Mixstead)

Ofsted inspections were seen by teachers as focusing on failure: 'It's a checking up, fault finding exercise,' 'Ofsted is nit picking,' 'Even if it was wonderful they would find the negative,' 'They're bound to find fault and after they do I shall feel crappy,' 'They're primed to look for the negative,' 'They have to find something wrong,' 'I'll only remember the negative,' 'They're trying to catch us out,' 'An Ofsted inspection makes you focus on failures, it is a degrowth experience,' 'Ofsted makes you criticize yourself more, which I think is a shame as teachers don't blow their own trumpet, and I think they should. They are being condemned for the things they do.' On a pre-inspection visit to one school by the RgI, the staff were given a 20 minute talk about the way in which a failing school would be identified and the procedures that needed to be adopted after that designation. 'It was as though they'd already decided', said one teacher. Letica (Lowstate), prior to her inspection, was

. . . just waiting to be criticized because that's what it has to be. . . . People I know have told me I'm a very good teacher but I don't feel it, and I certainly don't feel that I'm teaching as well as I used to, therefore I can't possibly be a good teacher, there's too much pressure and it can't change.

For Edith (Lowstate), there was the fear of either being sacked or not being reemployed. She was doing long term supply at the time of the inspection and was criticized for losing control of some of her pupils and for not having a good display. This occurred in one of her lessons, but in talking it through a week or so later, it appeared that inspectors had made at least nine visits to her classroom.

> I began to wonder what the headteacher was thinking about me and whether she though that I had caused the Key Stage 1 group to be down-graded. The way they came up to me and spoke to me made me feel like I'd really let everyone down, made me feel that I hadn't done things correctly. However, if I tell myself 7 out of 9 as satisfactory, I would have been walking with my head held high, given that I was a new teacher and being assessed for the first time. I was thinking of not coming back to teach again. I like the staff here and I like the children so I'd like to stay but now with these people saying this about me, I wondered what the head was thinking. Was she thinking of keeping me?

Helen (Cottingly) had similar feelings:

> I don't think I've got a guilt complex or anything, but if something was said about this class and it was obvious it was this class, I just keep thinking 'Am I going to feel good enough in my job afterwards to carry on?' 'Am I going to be able to face parents who see this report and still uphold my belief that I'm doing my best for them?' 'Am I a good enough teacher to teach your children?' And that worries me because I don't think I should feel that way because I think I am doing my best and I hope that if I wasn't achieving a good enough result I think somebody would have said so by now.

A term after her Ofsted inspection, Erica (Mixstead) seemed not only to have recovered but she had learnt some hard lessons as well as finding herself in a position to be able to assess the worth of an Ofsted approach.

> Having gone through the Ofsted experience, I just thought, 'No, I am not going to let anybody do that again'. The LEA visit is a different sort of an approach, it felt more like when I was at college. They are there to help you rather than just to pick up on everything. I know that Ofsted pick up on any good things that you do, but I think they are here to find out what you do wrong. The LEA inspector sat here with his clipboard as usual, and he was talking to the children, and he was asking them things. He was trying to get from them everything that Ofsted didn't do. I think he did more of a thorough job than Ofsted did, yet I was still relaxed. I think it is the air of authority, that matters. He introduced himself to the children and to me.

Rachael, her headteacher, points out why it is hard to take such criticism:

> It is very personal, because the job that we do is a personal job, us
> and 30 children, what could be more personal than that? I can't say it
> is the office junior's fault, or the computer's fault like many people can
> in their jobs, or lack of communications from above, teachers never
> use that one really, well I rarely hear that one. I don't think they blame
> me when it goes wrong, most times, but blame themselves for what
> has happened. We can't easily pass the buck as a teacher.

Teachers cultivate a 'persona of perfection' (A. Hargreaves, 1994, p. 149). At
the same time, they are aware that absolute and continuous perfection is un-
attainable. Sophie (Flately) commented: 'It's just slowly eroding away your confidence till you're beginning to doubt nearly everything that you do. You know
we're trying to be Mr and Mrs Perfectionist next week and it's impossible.' This
led, for some, to feelings of persecutory guilt, 'a self disappointment, a sense
of having done badly, fallen short, of having betrayed a personal ideal, standard or commitment' (A.F. Davies, 1989, p. 49). This guilt is exacerbated during
an Ofsted inspection (see Chapter 4). Instead of recognizing its unattainability,
the 'objective' grading of teachers also implies that teaching perfection exists.
In fact there is no consensus about a 'perfect' model for teaching, indeed ideas
as to what constitutes 'good teaching' have been shown to be linked to socio-
political and historical circumstance (Grace, 1985; Woods et al., 1997). The
lack of a generally agreed model, together with the dearth of qualitative feedback, led some teachers to wonder how they could possibly succeed. 'If they
would tell us how to do it, I'd do it, but they can't or won't' (Grace — Flately).

In such circumstances there is everything to lose and nothing to gain:

> If you are talking to a particular child and they suddenly start writing
> a lot, you think 'Is that right, have I done it right? Perhaps I said the
> wrong thing?' So I don't think it is much benefit at all. It just put
> everybody on edge, you could cut the atmosphere with a knife half
> the time. When I spoke to a governor he said, 'All the staff are very
> tense'. I said, 'Well, do you really expect us to be relaxed?' He said, 'I
> would have thought by Wednesday you would have relaxed.' I don't
> know what they think we are! And one of the inspectors said, which
> put my back up, 'Mondays are usually very tense, Tuesdays are relax-
> ing and Wednesday or Thursday is when they really start to slip up.' I
> thought, 'That's what you are waiting for.' (Kay — Mixstead)

> The assumption is that teachers are inadequate. That's why I don't
> like this, it stinks!!! It thrives on inadequacy. What does this do for
> teachers' self-esteem? Why do I have to have all these people checking
> up on me? . . . I just want to do my job — the job I used to love, I was
> there till 6 o'clock every night until I had my kids. Even then I used to
> take work home and kids home, take kids out to do the netball team.

> I loved it, because people trusted me and I felt good about things. I don't feel good about anything I do anymore. (Naomi — Morghouse)

Deputy heads, often the creative force behind curriculum innovation, were not exempt from this feeling. Toni for example, felt 'not a failure but inadequate . . . I now watch my back the whole time'.

Conclusion

In summary, there were significant value differences between Ofsted and teachers with regard to:

Knowledge

Ofsted Values
- Prescribed National Curriculum
- Controlled National Curriculum
- Emphasis on Products
- Subject-based curriculum
- Systematization, Standardization, Uniformity

Teacher Values
- Negotiated National Curriculum
- Flexible and Autonomous Practices
- Emphasis on Process
- Child-centred, Holistic, Integrative
- Differences, Diversity

Pedagogy

Ofsted Values
- Transmissional
- Behaviourist
- Formal
- Examination
- Instant performance

Teacher Values
- Creative
- Constructivist Learning Theory
- Informal Contexts
- Support
- Learning takes time

Assessment (of pupils and teachers)

Ofsted Values
- Formal
- Quantitative
- Standardized
- Periodic tests
- Hierarchical Examination

- Simplicity

Teacher Values
- Informal
- Qualitative
- Localized
- Continuous
- Collective Engagement, Self-Assessment
- Complexity

Culture

Ofsted Values	**Teacher Values**
• Competition and Individualism	• Collegiality
• Detachment	• Involvement
• Blame	• Support
• Managerialism	• Professionalism
• Control	• Self-Regulation
• Consumer	• Producer

We argue that these value differences permeated the way in which inspections were conducted and how they were seen by inspectors and teachers, though they might have interpreted the others' actions as incompetence or inefficiency. The teachers seem to be in a different world from the inspectors represented in Chapter 1. The latter implied a consensus developed in their inspections, but there is no sign of it here, quite the reverse in fact. The question has to be asked if the teachers' objections were simply a result of not liking being inspected, and perhaps of having their shortcomings discovered. But most of these teachers did not have too many shortcomings to worry about — all the schools and most of the teachers received satisfactory or good reports. Most were experienced and hardened professionals, with a similar basic aim to that of Ofsted, that is of educational improvement. They would be very interested in policies and practices that would yield such improvement — but as they understood it to be. It is in the interpretation that the two part company, for teachers could not accept the Ofsted definition of knowledge, the accompanying recommendations for pedagogy, the managerialist approach to assessment, the distancing of themselves from colleagues and pupils and the culture of blame and failure. Nor is it simply a matter of adequacy or validity, but rather different definitions of validity, since one's view of what constitutes real, meaningful knowledge dictates the methods employed.

Another possibility is that the thoughts and feelings expressed here are largely figments of the teachers' imaginations — pre-inspection worries about what *might* happen — rather like a visit to the dentist (potentially painful, and to be avoided if possible, but ultimately in one's own best interests). Some of the reactions are anticipation certainly, but teachers' views were well founded, being based on material derived from the public and educational media, personal contacts, pre-inspection 'MOTs' and papers, and other schools' experiences and reports. Teachers' views are interpretations, certainly, and some of them may be a result of misunderstanding an inspector's words or actions. On the evidence presented here, a large number seem well founded. Whatever the case, their constructions of meaning are real for the teachers — and real in their consequences (Thomas, 1928).

We come back, therefore, to the argument that there is a basic clash of values here. And it is a conflict where teachers are in the weaker position.

They are under examination in a disciplinary exercise, where their humanistic morality has been replaced by one centred on technology. We have seen a number of comments here about teachers feeling that they were losing control of their own classrooms, and their very selves. Their whole lives, in effect, were colonized by the Ofsted process, as we discuss in the following chapter.

Notes from the Field (3)
Tuesday — Acclimatization Day

Support staff had been quizzed by inspectors about their timetables and the children had been good all day, even at lunchtime when the inspectors ate with them. More 'great maths investigations' had been missed and teachers with a number of responsibility 'hats' were having to switch modes to engage in interviews with inspectors one after the other. Others were pleased with themselves for not worrying about it the previous night, enjoying the evening and going to bed late. Pleased that 'today had gone well and that the feedback on yesterday's lessons had been more than good.' The inspectors themselves are examined. Evelyn thought 'They were approachable, talkable and the feedback was good because they were a particularly humane team' but Aileen thought one of them was 'severe.' Their encounters are dissected, 'There's a slight adrenaline surge as they come in. It feels right, I still feel calm, the children are responding well and it's a good atmosphere in the room. It was just like having another teacher in the room for she was talking to the children and helping.' However, others felt differently particularly when the children let them down. 'I wanted to kill Stephen. By the time I'd explained the problem he'd done it. I told them to make up their own. I hate them today. They played up during my Tudor class lesson. There was chewing gum all over the place, they were complaining about each other. Through clenched teeth I intoned "stop it." One child started making faces during music. I glared but decided not to stop the lesson. I thought "you horrors, you've shafted me." I told them I was disappointed with them and sent them home without a smile.' The inspectors were considered by this teacher as poor evaluators. 'He stayed for an hour in the history, didn't look at the displays or history work, just asked the children questions about the colour of the historical figures' tights and to name some Tudor battles.'

The head appears and asks for names of children to show off design and technology tomorrow and those who had had bad days decline her request emphatically, with a heightened emphasis to show their distaste, but conform later. As the daily stories subside, Amy asks Angelina for help with RE and the head again recounts a positive comment from the RgI, 'You must be proud of the school.' By seven minutes past four they have all returned again to the scenes of the action to prepare again for the next day or to be examined by inspectors about their posts of responsibilities. 'I couldn't answer any of the questions, "Why is there no instrument teaching here? Have you any recordings of pupils composing? How can you assess music in the school? Why hadn't the coordinator's report got any success criteria e.g.: for buying a CD player?." She didn't give me a chance to talk about resources. She had a long list of questions she rattled at me. I couldn't get a word in.'

It went better for others, 'An OK interview. He was clued in. He liked the classroom and the class work.' Some encounters were with sympathetic inspectors. 'She wanted me to tell her all the positive points. There was ample opportunity to make a response. There were no trick questions. It was searching but she gave me some positive comments back.' Some took control of the encounters, 'He didn't know about the wildlife garden. I had to sell myself and science. He listened a lot. He had a form and wrote in three or four parts but he had no batting order. He let me go left and right. I kidnapped him. I'd got it together because of the number of job applications I've made.'

As the evening wore on — at about 5 p.m. — I carefully made my way round the school wary of intervening in the process. I found a group in one room chatting and telling stories. 'My husband and dad — down from Scotland to help with the cooking — expected me to come home at lunchtime or after school in a real state. Instead I walked in at 6.00 and just said 'one day over. It's in the hands of the gods.'

I become the focus for discussion 'You lucky bugger sitting in the staffroom on Monday all calm and relaxed writing notes drinking coffee while we're having all the inspectors at us. Wait till Friday. We're going to put you in a class.'

Chapter 3

The Colonization of Teachers' Lives, Selves and Work

Ofsted inspectors' power derives partly from government legitimacy, and partly from the 'knowledge' that Ofsted accumulates. Lee and Fitz (1997, p. 49) argue that Ofsted

> not merely holds and controls information, but via the process of analysis and publication configures a powerful discourse in education. The central database leaves it in a strong position as custodians of 'knowledge' with the ability to reproduce and reformulate that knowledge in policy making.

The form of power exercised by Ofsted inspectors, we argue, is an example of what Foucault (1977) calls 'disciplinary power'. It seeks to produce well ordered organizations, and efficient, productive and disciplined people. This power, however, is not overt or 'held', as in sovereign power. Rather,

> it is exercised through its invisibility; at the same time it imposes on those whom it subjects a principle of compulsory visibility. In discipline it is the subjects who have to be seen. Their visibility assures the hold of power that is exercised over them. It is the fact of being constantly seen that maintains the disciplined individual in his subjection. (Ibid., pp. 202–3)

Nonetheless, if for much of the time invisible, it can at any time be made most visible and public, since inspectors have the power to fail teachers and schools, threatening the survival of both. Given the existing state of low morale and anxiety within the profession, owing to the 'discourse of derision' that has been directed at them (see Wallace, 1993, Woods et al., 1997), this is a very real threat, though it might be carried out with only a very small minority. This is a typical strategy of colonizers — making an example of a few to encourage the majority.

Consequently, while inspectors may only be in a school for less than a week, their influence permeates all aspects of school and teachers' lives, for a great deal of time, and cannot be avoided. In the year preceding the inspection some of the staff room notice boards were dominated by large school development plans, details of monitoring targets, absence statistics and school curriculum programmes. The invisibility of Ofsted inspectors except for a brief three or four days and their exercise of power is matched by the extent to which teachers' whole lives have become visible. A. Hargreaves (1994, p. 109) has remarked on how in recent years teachers' work has become colonized by the increased demands for administration, the most noticeable example of this being where

> the private, informal, 'back regions' of teachers' working lives are taken over by administrative purposes, converting them into public, formal 'front regions' (Goffman, 1959). In this way, configurations of time and space that used to mark a domain of private relaxation and relief increasingly mark a domain of public business and supervision.

The 'back regions' are moments such as the non-teaching period, lunch times and breaks and informal times. By transferring them to front of stage, and making them 'directed time' or otherwise consuming them, colonization makes visible 'what had hitherto been the private plans, thoughts, reflections and intentions of the subjects . . . what has previously been private, spontaneous and unpredictable becomes public, controlled and predictable' (A. Hargreaves, 1994, p. 112). 'We are witnessing', Hargreaves (Ibid. p. 113) argues, 'the growing administrative colonization of teachers' time and space'.

But the Ofsted colonization is even more penetrative and pervasive than this. 'You're working full time plus with the National Curriculum, now it's full time plus, plus for Ofsted, so where is your time coming from?' (Aileen-Lowstate) It comes from teachers' lives outside as well as inside school. Colonization affects teachers' identities and their domestic lives, as well as their professional roles and the workplace. Whole lives are taken over by the Ofsted discourse. This discourse serves both to reinforce power, and to encourage conformity, by establishing a 'regime of truth'. This is not truth in any absolute sense, but one specific to the discourse, one characterized by managerialism and technification (epitomized in the Ofsted 'Handbook'), and which serves to control and to regulate. It might be contrasted with 'professionalism', an alternative regime of truth which it replaces, deeming it outmoded. Foucault (1980, p. 133) argues that ' "Truth" is linked in circular relation with systems of power which produce and sustain it, and to effects of power which it induces and which extend it.' Thus, some teachers may internalize this particular regime of truth, and even claim to be enhanced by it. But their level of awareness might not rise above that of particular regimes, and they may be exhibiting a form of false consciousness (Densmore, 1987; Wilcox and Gray, 1996).

In this way, colonization can become self-operable. If the gaze of the inspectors is felt to be inescapable and continuous, the subject 'assumes responsibility for the constraints of power; he makes them play spontaneously upon himself; he inscribes in himself the power relation in which he simultaneously plays both roles; he becomes the principle of his own subjection' (Foucault, 1977, pp. 202–3). Thus, school development plans (SDP), for example, which might ostensibly appear to be empowering products of autonomous and independent organizations, can be a means by which schools are brought under increasing control. Inspectors need not be present for SDPs to be constructed in line with their specifications (see Troman, 1997a).

Other features of colonization for which there is evidence either here in our research or elsewhere are: exploitation of teachers' conscientiousness and sense of industry (Campbell and Neill, 1994b); teachers being represented as inferior, lacking or 'in deficit' (Ball, 1990a; Wallace, 1993); the fact that, to many teachers, Ofsted inspectors are foreigners, in the sense that they are driven by a different set of values with which they themselves do not identify (Woods and Jeffrey, 1996b; and see Chapter 1); the colonizers' claim that they are acting in the best interests of all, when they represent sectional interests (Woods and Wenham, 1994); the fact that there may be some benefits experienced by some teachers. Some individuals may feel enhanced (Woods at al., 1997), and others may find new roles for themselves (Webb and Vulliamy, 1996). Current educational practices are evaluated with new perspectives, and new practices may be developed which in time may be appreciated. But these benefits are outweighed by the overall effect.

'Discipline', Foucault (1977, p. 139) writes, 'is a political anatomy of detail'. We need to study the minutiae of social action to show how the discipline works to produce its effects. Since power is 'exercised rather than possessed', and is 'the overall effect of its strategic positions' (Ibid. p. 27), it would be a mistake to concentrate on those at the top. Rather, we should examine how discourses work to produce their effects. In this chapter, therefore, we consider how the teachers of our research have been affected by Ofsted. Their whole selves have been colonized — their lives in and out of school, their relationships, their bodies, their beliefs, and their very personalities.

The first stage in this transformation is normal ways of maintaining the self beginning to fragment. Diane (Morghouse) received a strong hint from an inspector to the effect that 'I'm the one in power, you're going to do what I say.' The language of targets, forecasts and evidence become a dominating discourse in teachers' work. Teachers began to do strange things, as when Deena, at the same school, 'found that I was actually filling in my topic forecast for our reception children with Attainment Targets and Levels. Why, did I do that? That's stupid. I began to think, "Am I getting caught up in it, am I doing this for them? Would I have done it anyway?" ' The process can lead to a suppression of the real self, and the appearance of some unpleasant character traits. Grace (Flately) told us 'Sleeplessness leads to stress for me and then I can be tactless, resentful, snarly, flippant and unpredictable. I can be seen at my worst. My body language changes. It's not really me but I'm angry when I do it. Things come out all wrong.' Eventually, Carol (Trafflon) fears that she will lose contact with reality and become an Ofsted clone:

In the end it's actually going to kill something within you as you won't do anything interesting and you won't be stimulated, you'll just be boring people talking about Ofsted. That's the ultimate worry, that you will just lose contact with reality.

We consider in this chapter how teachers lose contact with one reality, and how their whole worlds are colonized by Ofsted. Chapter 4 will then examine one trend prefigured in this activity, that of teachers' deprofessionalization; while Chapter 5 will look at how, in spite of this, teachers are managing to cope.

Colonizing Life

Ofsted inspections lead to a suspension of life. The full involvement of a primary teacher's self in the job has been noted (Nias, 1989). Nor is it anything new to see the merging of the public and private lives in teachers' work (Mills, 1959; Miller, 1996). That said, it would appear important in the management of stress of teachers' work and for feelings of general fulfilment, that a balance between public and private be sustained. In recent years, that delicate balance has become more and more disturbed as the increasing pressures have intruded upon the private sphere. The Ofsted inspection threatens to disturb this balance further, eating into, and in some instances eroding, teachers' family life, leisure activities and social life. Their lives, and their capabilities as teachers, are in consequence, they feel, being diminished. Carol (Trafflon) used to

> just go around and visit friends because work didn't have any claims on your time, they would say 'stay to tea or whatever'. That's stopped, because when the day ends you don't think, 'Ah, 3.30 I can go home', you just think 'God! Now I've got millions of things to do before I can get to bed at night'. . . . I used to go to the theatre a lot. . . . That's one of the biggest things I miss about the workload that we've got now is that I don't actually have time for any interests of my own and that's what I used to feed off. . . . These interests actually made me more interesting to the children because I had the time to go to museums and I used to enjoy picking up postcards and thinking 'that would be quite useful'. I feel trapped sometimes, it's just like a roller coaster at the moment, you just don't ever stop. . . . I feel oppressed but I've just got resigned to it.

Toni (Trafflon) feels

> this heaviness when I enter my home that sometimes my home is my prison because I'm there and I have to work and I refuse invitations. If I had somebody else in my house, I could get rid of a little bit of that feeling of frustration of my day. All my waking moments when I am at

work are filled with work. If I'm out with friends, I forget work but when I'm home I can't forget it because I'm thinking all the time, 'when I've cooked this meal I'll watch television for half an hour then I must get on with this work'.

Corrine (Trafflon), a single parent, goes to bed at 2 a.m.,

then I'm dead; I want to go to sleep. In the morning I'm telling my eldest one, 'the alarm's going, get up'. I don't want him to be in charge. I'm the mum but the way it is I have shown him the things to do, have a bath, put the kettle on. I tell him all these things and I think 'my God, I'm terrible, my God I'm terrible'. And then the little one is saying 'Why don't you come earlier, why do you have to go to the child minder first, why can't I go to school directly?' I'm really getting angry and I end up saying, 'That's it, off to bed; I've cancelled the swimming. All those things I used to get home to on certain days like swimming with my children every week, that's gone. I'm here in school, trying to improve all the children's education but I'm neglecting mine; they're suffering. It shouldn't be like that. The only reason I got into primary teaching was to help them and have more time with my children.

Kayleigh (Mixstead) was still sitting up in bed with maths literature late at night when her husband begged her to stop. 'It's almost as if you feel, you haven't got time to sleep.' Aileen recounted how she had 'twice set the alarm off in the house by wandering around in the middle of the night whilst marking and planning'. Ofsted even pervades teachers' dreams. Glen (Flately) dreamt that inspectors were digging up his back garden. He also found himself

on a big parade ground, being inspected, marching up and down, and the bloke was shouting 'about turn, about turn' but he couldn't make us do what he wanted us to do and in the end he gave the front man a paintbrush and he had to walk along with it held up in the air. We all followed this paintbrush off the square and then everything was all right. This was to do with my Art Coordinator's post.

Kay (Mixstead) crept into the kitchen to do her school work. Veronica (Trafflon) stayed at school to avoid working at home so that the latter did not interfere with her preparation, but she set her 'alarm at 6 a.m. during the holidays to get things done'.

Even arrangements about a family death had to be made around school preparations:

Would you believe that just before that happened my mother died, and I had to stay at my post! Oh dear, that was a trial! We buried her on a Saturday because Saturday was a convenient day, so it did not interfere with my work. (Reen — Mixstead)

Reen's husband who lectures at a London University argues that 'it is difficult to keep a sense of balance while Reen does so much work at home. She is busy on school work from 8 in the morning to 9 in the evening'. When Kirsty's (Mixstead) son came down to do his paper round she was already downstairs doing school work, 'I just don't believe it' he said 'you're crazy'. She thought he was probably right. Her husband wanted her to go and work in Tesco's to cut down on her extra school work. Rita (Mixstead) had her half term colonized and relations were, 'not too good, because my husband has taken the week off. We were going to the coast and all those sort of things. He's stuck at home painting windows at the moment and in rather a sad mood'. Kay and her husband had won a holiday competition:

> We decided that we both needed a break and he decided on half term and I just burst into tears and said; 'No.' He had obviously been thinking about it all day, and I had a blinding headache anyway and I just said; 'No!' I said; 'Any other half term I would have jumped at it.' He said; 'Well two days, then.' and I said; 'Well I don't think I can even do that.' He said; 'Just the two of us.' It sounded lovely. So he is not very happy with me because I said, 'No way can I go away for a week.'

She didn't take her two days. Colonization works here not only through the direct demands that are made on her time, but from exhaustion caused by the concentration of demands, that, for example, have eaten up all spare moments of the school day and affects personal relations as the space for other engagements diminishes, as Roger (Mixstead) exemplifies, 'I had nothing to say to her [his partner]. I had no reason to smile, and all in all it was a completely wasted six hour evening.'

Rebecca (Flately) admitted that 'I don't have time for the problems of others at home because I'm so tired.' Carol (Trafflon) lived on her own but felt conflicting responsibilities towards her family. 'My brother came to stay the last week of the holidays, and when I say I didn't want him to come it was because I just knew I was going to be busy.' Bronwyn's (Cottingly) husband told us:

> If you've got families it conflicts with the professionals' code of dedication to the job and that puts too much pressure on. I'm fed up to the hind teeth with it. It's ceaseless, it's day in day out, week in week out now, gearing up. . . . They won't admit to being torn between family and work because they're professional people. It's up to the spouses, to give them support, which we have done but there are times when you say, 'don't do it', and the cry is 'I've got to, it's got to be done.'

Simpler resolutions were adopted in Nancy's (Morghouse) family, 'He left for a day or two a week prior to Ofsted just to get out of the way.'

If a school holiday came close before the inspection the teachers spent most of their time in the school during that break. Reen (Mixstead) was in school for the whole of the half term prior to the inspection except for two hours at the hairdresser's. She noted 'how the people there (at the hairdressers) seemed happy and how slow the pace was. I was offered some magazines but opened my blue file instead'. Teachers with young children escaped from the stress a little at home because of the demands of their children, but it didn't stop them staying very late in school and making other arrangements for their infants to be supervised in the meantime. However, family support was sometimes more tangible. At Cottingly, 30 per cent of the teachers brought their family in to help them. One husband, an assistant education authority director, perched on a ladder and stuck pictures on to a high wall with blu-tac. Another, a business man, sawed wood for a science lesson, and another cut out pictures. Daughters coloured in displays. Sunday was not a day of rest if you were being Ofsteded, but it was still a family affair — albeit devoted to Ofsted.

Some teachers and relatives put off hospital visits and operations. Ruth (Flately) was involved in technical support at Flately and when she was asked if she would do some workshops during Ofsted week she cancelled an important gynaecological appointment 100 miles away. Some teachers were convinced that some of their family resisted illnesses until the event was over for they became ill soon afterwards. Katrina's (Mixstead) 72-year-old mother postponed an operation until the inspection was over, which made Katrina wonder 'what was happening to her life'. Most teachers put things like this second to Ofsted. Esther ironically asked, 'Oh, did we have a holiday? I don't remember. Oh no, I remember now, yes, my mother was dying and that was a bit hectic.'

Household responsibilities were re-arranged for the week. Children in one family were left to go to school on their own in the mornings for the first time because the husband and wife teachers in the same school wanted to be in school very early during the inspection, and arrangements were made by them to visit Macdonald's on most nights. Arguments were greater in this family during the period leading up to the inspection. Rose (Mixstead) asked her husband not to be busy the weekend prior to the inspection and filled the freezer with food. Most meals were prepared prior to the week in most households. Rosa (Flately) had 'take aways' every night. Child care arrangements were altered; ex-husbands supervised the children or a husband altered his work routines to deal with the children, and housework was left undone. A fathering role was dispensed with by one teacher for the week and the new baby was hardly seen. In spite of intentions to the contrary, Rebecca and Ruth (Flately) cancelled their aerobics class during the inspection week because they were too tired. Shula, at the same school, stopped doing meditation which normally helped her relax, 'I am too stressed to do it', and Bronwyn (Cottingly) postponed a birthday celebration with her new husband.

The multi-dimensional and delicately balanced nature of women's lives in particular was upset in that their 'triple shift' of home maker, mother, and professional careerist (Acker, 1994) was disturbed (a number of these teachers had responsibilities for ageing relatives, adding a fourth 'shift'). On top of that, some partners found it difficult to understand why the women teachers gave so much time to their work. Diane (Morghouse) greeted her husband with,

> 'Hello — how are you?' Same as you would a stranger. That's sad, isn't it? I did warn him before the beginning of the school term, 'I'm going to be desperately busy till the end of January', but he doesn't know what's going on.

Some of the teachers' children were going through difficult times as teenagers, doing 'A' levels, leaving for college, or suffering from medical conditions. Kay had two sick daughters, and 'the older one is giving me a lot of grief at the moment'. Some of the teachers were supporting male partners who were having work problems of their own. Clare's husband, for example, a lecturer in computer studies, had just been redeployed to another college:

> He's under the most shocking stress, terrible; he's up at 4 every morning because he can't sleep; he's become a complete insomniac so I'm not going to go home and talk to either of them about my Ofsted problems. I've got to go home and try and be the calm one — a joke!

Colonization marginalizes these extra responsibilities, and at the same time heightens the feelings attached to them, for work not only encroaches upon the responsibilities but the dominance of work doesn't allow time to resolve the emotions that are connected with family relations or allow teaching to ameliorate them:

> I had a bad Sunday, a bad bout of depression partly to do with home and partly thinking about Ofsted. Something triggers it off at home and you think; 'Oh, I have got school tomorrow', and what have I got to look forward to at school, just this thing hanging over me, this Ofsted hanging over me. School work to do on Sunday, that sort of thing.

Keith (Mixstead), a newly qualified teacher, sacrificed his leisure occupation as a Civilian Instructor in the Air Training Corps. Kirsty, at the same school, cancelled a lunch date during the half term break prior to the inspection but did remember to phone her daughter and wish her luck in her driving test unlike Diane (Morghouse) who forgot. However, Kirsty told her husband that she could not engage in a social event during the weekend prior to the inspection in spite of the fact that her husband worked away from home all week. One boyfriend living some 90 miles away had to forego seeing his girlfriend teacher Freda (Cottingly) for three consecutive weekends and the relationship broke up soon after Ofsted. Her flatmates could not appreciate her situation either and when she became responsible for doing the only class assembly during her inspection where she felt she was representing the whole school the isolation became very apparent:

> The people who live with me knew I was stressed, but I don't think they fully appreciated the hell that everyone was going through. They thought everyone was making a bit of a fuss about nothing and my boyfriend was the most guilty of anybody.

Even mature teachers were not immune to anxiety about relationships. Bronwyn (Cottingly) got home at 6 o'clock on the Sunday prior to her inspection and fantasized that her new husband was leaving:

> It was the last straw. When I got home, he was locking up the gate, taking the dog for a walk. He was abandoning me. It was terrible really. I got into the house and I went into the garden and I saw the washing on the line — 'Oh my God! . . . perhaps I should take the washing down.' I went into the kitchen and started to clear up quickly feeling guilty and I had to stop myself and say 'Hang on, do you know what you're doing?' I was really quite frightened by the state I got into that Sunday.

Colonizing the Body

> You drive yourself mad to be perfect, it's just endless grey hairs and early graves. (Letica — Lowstate)

Stress is not uncommon in schools, especially since the late 1980s (Sandbrook, 1996; Brimblecombe et al., 1995; Wilcox and Gray, 1996; Woods et al., 1997), but it is compounded by colonization (Casey, 1995). Teachers in schools that received excellent reports still experienced high levels of stress. Freda (Cottingly) found it exhausting:

> I don't think it's right that we have been put through what we've been put through. I wonder how many other jobs are put through the hell that we've been put through in that way. . . . it's a tough enough job anyway.

Stress is further exacerbated by the 'discourse of derision' mentioned earlier. Harry (Morghouse) left for a new post just three weeks before their Ofsted inspection. He spoke of the pressures from the outside:

Look at what happens to a school that doesn't get a good report. In our Local Education Authority every school that has its Ofsted has a press release in the local paper. There are programmes on television, for example the Panorama programme about Ofsted last week. This was a major talking point in the staffroom the day after; it wouldn't necessarily have been so a year ago. The whole profile of inspection has been raised, hasn't it, by Ofsted? Inspections have always happened, you had an HMI team in and it probably had the same powers as an Ofsted team, but it was never as demoralizing.

The teachers all admitted, even those who paced themselves, that they could not have continued at the pace they were working for much longer than the period of the inspection. They saw the Ofsted process as an event which had an end to it, and consequently they were willing to make personal sacrifices until the event was over. Cloe (Trafflon) said her main expenses at the moment were 'prescriptions and masking tape'. Some of them resorted to drugs and other comforting intakes such as food. Others resisted the drugs out of principle but nevertheless their engagement was not diminished. Stress and drugs were connected. Veronica, at the same school, explained the relationship, for her, between engagement, stress and drugs. 'Most people under stress eat more but it's too much trouble to eat. I'd sooner have a cigarette and a cup of tea.' Veronica's mother noticed her need for alcohol.

> When my mother's gone home, I can start drinking again. She said to me quite mildly: 'You know, dear, I do think you ought to stop drinking. Well no, not stop drinking but I do think you ought to cut it down.' So I said, 'Oh yes, I just feel in need of a drop, that's all, Mum. I get on fine. I'm not getting drunk or anything.' 'Oh no, no, dear, I know', but she said, 'You're having a couple every time you come home.' So I've been struggling not to. There'll be a quick swig after we've finished Friday and then I'll suck a mint to go indoors.

Aileen (Lowstate), after critical comments during a practice inspection admitted that 'I got home last night and I downed two gin and tonics straight away, cried and moaned at Alec, my husband.' Letica, at the same school, didn't drink but resorted to drugs. 'I've just got to feel on top of it. I can't go under, I can't really. I'm going to take some calming tablets. . . . Yes, I'll get through it. You've got to feel ready and prepared.' They appeared to work. Kayleigh (Mixstead) got migraines and needed to 'put blinkers on to stay healthy'. Grace (Flately) said 'I've never taken a tranquilliser in my life but I could not go for two weeks with the fear that I would not sleep so I'll be round to my sister's to get some.'

Kay (Mixstead) resorted to food, 'I eat! That is all I do; I eat. I have probably put on three quarters of a stone. I get to a state sometimes if I am really low where I eat everything, regardless of whether I really like it or not. It is an awful way to be, because you feel so stupid; you can see yourself putting on weight.' Carol and Clare (Trafflon) immersed themselves in food but not with any great satisfaction. 'We had this conversation which was non stop and I thought I am turning into a dustbin. It was obscene. I ate and chewed like a cow eating fodder. It was fuel; both Carol and I were just stuffing our faces and we talked for two hours non stop in between getting extra cups of coffee. It was manic. I've never ever had that before; we just had to have the food because we were talking about Ofsted and we didn't notice it. It was fuel for thinking.'

Nancy (Morghouse) went to therapy for assistance. Later on she 'used hypnosis tapes to help me sleep'. Lucy (Lowstate) had a hypnotist friend who advised her 'If you start to get anxious just take a really deep breath; don't say anything just breathe. The other thing you can do in your head is, shrink the inspector into a plant.' Illnesses were related to stress and the relief of stress. Frank (Cottingly) suffered from a stomach disorder during Ofsted and had to go to the doctor's. Gayle (Flately) had flu and George, at the same school, had a throat infection, lost his voice and his deputy Shula had gumboils. After the inspection was the worst time for many teachers with illnesses emerging from suppressed states of engagement, as Esther (Lowstate) observed, 'All my glands are infected and my throat's infected and inside my nose is all infected and I have these horrible cold sores. When I get really run down, things like this happen.'

Colonizing Beliefs

The Ofsted colonization undermined teachers' belief in the work ethic, and challenged their vocational commitment.

There is strong evidence that teachers have been working extremely hard, especially during the intensification of primary teachers' work that has taken place over the last few years (Campbell and Neill, 1994a; Brimblecombe et al., 1995; Sandbrook, 1996; Troman, 1997b; Woods and Jeffrey, 1996b). The amount of work gradually increased as the inspection approached. The work ethic to which they subscribed led them to believe that hard work would result in a successful outcome for them and the school. However, as the headteacher of Lowstate observed, 'They have taken it all on board but they're being pushed down. They absorbed all the planning, forecasts and policy development. They do all this hard work to be knocked down.' Letica (Lowstate) was in a criticized department but was not singled out: 'You don't know whether any written comments were about you. . . . Therefore, it's really not much use to you.' Aileen was considered a good teacher but was in a criticized department:

It's made me think, if they can do something that is so obnoxious and so demoralizing then you think, 'Where are we going, what is it all for at the end of the day? It's not for the kids, because if it is, leaving us

questioning what the whole process is about, detracts from the learning and teaching that we are doing. . . . Is there very much good about
us in that report? No. So the careers of a lot of us who tried very hard
are left feeling 'God!' . . . It just wasn't worth it, all that hassle for a
report so bland that we can't recognize our school — and to be just
told we are 'satisfactory'.

She couldn't understand how her department, Key Stage 1, with good SATs
results for the year, could have been criticized whereas Key Stage 2 with poor
SATs results were applauded. 'I mean for the school in general it was a good
report, but you were scrambling around to find anything good about our
department when actually our results were good. We can't understand why we
were criticized. We cannot understand where it's going to end.' A belief in
hard work had been undermined.

Their feeling of trust was also diminished. Power (1994) argues that
accountability in public services has become a substitute for trust, and that
certainly seems to be born out here. Robina, a recently appointed head of
department in Flatley school, felt this after her department had been criticized
just as she was getting to grips with its problems,

What game is really being played and why? They're here all the time
pushing for more and more and making you feel that you can't achieve,
questioning your capability. I think that's why I went home and thought
about resigning, because I thought that there is a big question-mark
over my head the whole time as to how capable I am of doing this
job. You can't work like that because there's got to be a sense of trust,
if you've been appointed and been given a job and if you feel that the
powers-that-be just don't trust you to do the job properly and then
they home in here like some kind of old-fashioned police — it's awful,
it's really horrible.

Colonizing Individuality

Individualism in primary teaching is seen as the cause of a lack of coherence
and continuity in primary schools (Alexander, 1992) and, when related to
autonomy, as an excuse to avoid any observation of their practice (Hargreaves,
1980). However, A. Hargreaves (1994), via Lukes and Balzac, makes a distinc-
tion between individualism and individuality.

For Lukes the first implies 'anarchy and social atomization'. The second
implies 'personal independence and self realisation'. *Individualism*
leads to the relaxation of social unity — the traditional concern of
sociological writers like Durkheim. But the extinction of *individuality*

(perhaps in the name of removing individualism) creates only a spurious unity; surrender to public opinion. (Ibid., p. 178 — author's italics)

The developments in collaborative policy development in primary schools in recent years (Nias et al., 1989) and the introduction of the National Curriculum has ensured a greater balance between the individuality of the teacher and the corporate aims of schools. However individuality was being threatened by the boost that Ofsted was giving to the process of technicization and the increased corporatism that resulted from the schools' desires to achieve success in Ofsted terms.

Technicization

Technicization is a feature of modernity, of efficiency, productivity and prosperity. Braverman (1974) argues that, in order to increase these features, workers' experience is continually refined in a reductionist manner which results in despoiling, the separation of management and workers, planning from execution, and mental from manual work. Technical rationality (Habermas, 1972), as the basis for judgment and planning, has become a feature of our lives within organizations and social life (A. Hargreaves, 1994, p. 32). Technicisation aids colonization since it is all pervasive. It also depersonalizes and dehumanizes, casting teachers as resources to be used and distancing 'managers from the personal and human consequences of their actions' (Ball, 1994, p. 63).

> I do feel very much that our autonomy has been taken away. I think one of the great things about primary schools was that they were different and now we are all becoming the same like the American or the French system, where all the schools are running the same procedures. The individuality and the craziness of some teachers didn't affect the children badly. You read about these famous teachers who were absolute nut cases, completely off their trolleys really, but they had this enthusiasm and this way of getting things across. I just feel we are all becoming the same. . . . you could get a trained monkey to do it, but our own individual inputs as human beings and personalities are being lost in the quagmire of paper work and keeping to the statements of attainment and all that sort of stuff. (Cloe — Trafflon)

Angelina (Lowstate) calls it 'teaching for others':

> You're forever looking over your shoulder, filling in a form or flicking through the National Curriculum to see which bit this lesson pertains to. Teaching has always been a never-ending job, you could fill 24 hours a day doing it, but in the past you were doing it for the love of doing it, because you wanted to do it to improve the children. Now

you are doing it because somebody is saying, 'Have you filled in this record card, what position or level is this child at? What assessment are you going to do to show me the evidence? Where is your evidence?'

Veronica (Trafflon) was told she was wrong when she defended her use of apparatus for her maths: 'They're not looking for individuality. They're looking for conformity.' Teachers interpreted inspectors as 'wanting to see a quiet controlled classroom'. Veronica avoided risk taking activities and spontaneity:

I got excited about an activity about liquids and measuring and suggested to the group that we made ice of the coloured water and then measured it. Suddenly I realized that an inspector was behind me and I turned and said 'not while you're here'.

A postholder felt that the inspector

. . . wanted me to go and teach each teacher to teach Maths exactly the same way . . . because then the children don't have to adapt each year. Well I don't think it hurts children to adapt each year because I think they learn different ways that way. If we all taught exactly the same way, how boring it would be for a start. (Enid — Mixstead)

All lesson plans, record keeping and policies were expected to use a standard framework and most of the schools ensured this was in place by the time the inspection team arrived, in spite of each school actually being a different institution, teaching different children whose needs differed depending on age, and teachers who taught in different ways.

I've written that policy the same way as everybody else has done but it's not couched in a way that I speak or I think or I believe, it's couched in such a way that it's not come from me. I'm not allowed to be me even in my maths policy statement. They might as well just write it down for me. . . . Are they trying to make us all clones so that in the end we're all the same and we all teach the same? I have visited schools and everyone's supposed to teach maths the same way. I find it quite scary. (Bronwyn — Cottingly)

The acceptance of differences in institutions provides a creative culture (Woods and Jeffrey, 1996b).

Why am I getting upset about these blooming people? They don't know the answer because everybody teaches differently. They teach differently. We all teach differently. I can't teach the way they teach or the way they were taught to teach, I've got to develop my own way of teaching. The way I speak to the children and everything is very different. (Tracy — Lowstate)

The head at Cottingly believed

in mix and match and I firmly believe that teachers can choose the best methods for them to communicate to the children. There are some teachers who can get across incredible things in an extremely formal way and fire and motivate the children, others are the exact opposite. The personality of the teacher and what they feel comfortable with is a very important factor because they've got to feel confident and competent with what they wish to put across.

The grading of teachers colonizes their individuality by ciphering them, reducing them to a number or category. Amy, who was given an excellent grade (see Chapter 2), agonised over whether to put the grading on her application form for new job,

because I don't think it defines me as a teacher because it has nothing to do with my practice. . . . I deplore the fact that they should employ me because these people came in, and give me a little number 1. I am what I have done all over the years. . . . Wherever I go I want to be judged by my merits, I want them to like me as a person, I want them to like my teaching, and not feel that I am going to say 'Well, you are lucky to have me because look what these silly people have said about me'.

For Shula (Flately) it was a feeling of displacement:

It's turning round and saying that the teacher in all of this is not important, that's what it is. It's saying 'well anybody can do it then', we're not particularly special to this particular time and place. It's this displacement thing again, we're not important. They're saying, 'if you have a particular model, you don't need anyone to interpret it for those children, there's no need for variable interaction because all children are the same — aren't they? You don't need the children to have different experiences and different people teaching them.'

Corporate Pressures

The change in school culture, which included the breaking of professional and humanistic attachments (see Chapter 2), also generated a move towards a corporate school approach stimulated by the desire to gain a satisfactory Ofsted report for the teachers' own professional survival and to satisfy the 'market'. It was done by maximizing collegial allegiances and school unity above individual approaches and interests.

Collegial Allegiances

In these circumstances teachers felt more responsible to their colleagues. In spite of the fact that

> people know that there's no direct comeback to them they genuinely feel, 'What if it's me that let's the team down and what if it's me that's picked up on'. In a small school like this you do know who it comes down to and if the report says something like, 'the Year 5 children weren't on task', it can be clear who are the people concerned. They are worrying that perhaps it's going to be them that lets the side down. (Harry — Morghouse)

Rachael, head teacher of Mixstead school, had been told by her local inspector to be a bit more positive about Ofsted with her staff for their sakes:

> I have a bit of a problem with any form of inspection, and yet I am aware that I am responsible for a number of other people's careers, so I can't just denigrate it. It is a dilemma. I find these people unnecessary, totally unnecessary. And yet I want the teachers to give of their best. I think I know what a good primary school is. I don't need some nut to drive up from a county over 100 miles away and tell me! However, I don't want to rub them up the wrong way. I haven't been cautious up until now, but I think now as the teachers are working towards it I will be more guarded in what I say because I want to make sure that they are going to survive this.

Head teachers may be constrained by their position and forced to adopt a corporate approach but it is also the case that newly qualified teachers have to live with the same constraints. Keith, at the same school, notes that the

> . . . obvious difference with teaching practice was that I was under pressure just for myself but in this thing it is the school that you are working for as well, so you have got to keep up, you don't want to fail, you don't want to get your colleagues into any trouble. So I won't be approaching it in exactly the same way. I don't think I will be able to sort of go my own way with Ofsted coming up, I think it is going to be a bit more of an act to act up to what is needed.

Individuals portray themselves as parts of a corporate body to the detriment of themselves as individuals:

At Key Stage 1 the staff are quite down at the moment because we didn't come out half as well as in the other staff so it becomes divisive. It's bound to happen because they keep on talking about the team being only as good as the weakest link. I keep thinking, 'I'm the weak link here, I'm going to let the others down' and obviously people are beginning to feel, 'Oh gosh I'm going to spoil it for Ofsted', so if you lose confidence you don't perform as well, so the whole thing escalates. (Aileen — Lowstate)

Guilt develops (see Chapter 4):

I'm feeling torn. You see the school is open on a Wednesday evening late, until 9 pm, so that we can come back or stay on if we want to. I just can't do it, you know it is not fair on my 12-year-old. I felt the pressure to come in during half term and although I probably would have done anyway, certainly these Wednesdays make me feel guilty. It has been put to us that the caretaker is being paid to keep the school open, and we ought to be here and I feel guilty because I can't do it. My colleague I work with has been staying on Wednesdays but she has got no family commitments at all, so yes I feel bad. (Katrina — Mixstead)

The formality of the Ofsted report and its support for corporatism through its reporting in departments disturbs the balance between school collegiality and individual performance.

I was just pissed off with the Ofsted because one of the inspectors took me aside and said, 'What you're doing is right', but then they are not evaluating individuals. However, the action plan was ambiguous and the fact that there was going to be INSET (In-Service Training for Teachers) for all of us meant I started to question my teaching methods and my philosophy so much so that I kept on asking people to come in and assess me and see what was happening. I can't work like that. I do believe if my practice was wrong, if something was wrong with my practice, I would want to be told but there is this undertone with which I can't cope. (Simca — Flately)

Aileen (Lowstate) found herself in the same position,

I don't agree with that expression, 'being tarred with the same brush'. I think we've all got to work together but I don't know. I know quite a few people who know that I'm in Key Stage 1, people I've taught with over the years, and they'll see the report and they'll say 'well, not very good in Key Stage 1'. I don't know what you do. I think it was unfair, it's depressing actually. I'd rather not dwell on it, I find it depressing for all of us in Key Stage 1.

School unity

Corporate policies have to be followed to satisfy an inspection. Letica (Lowstate) found that only certain approaches were acceptable in her school for an Ofsted inspection, a situation reminiscent of Alexander's (1995) criticism of the power of orthodoxies:

> Of course I'm not allowed to teach them the way I want to teach them, the way I think they ought to be taught and that is another added constraint because I can't perform at my best if I can't do what I know is best. Everything's got to be done according to the school policy so down comes my particular phonics frieze, up goes this one simply because the way the letters are written because this is 'how we do it here'. It's not as colourful as my other one, the children are not as interested in it. Ofsted must see that we're doing is what it says in our policy document. Well I'm hoping that I can slip it out again when it's over.

Reen (Mixstead) admitted that she totally changed her practice to fit within the school's published policies even though she had the governors and parents tacit support for her SATs' revision approach with Year 6:

> The parents are staggered at the high standard these children have to reach. So I try and cover 100 per cent of the test requirements. I can't do it, too much before the Ofsted, because the inspectors will say to the children, 'Is this the way you normally teach?' and they will say; 'No'. I can't have Ofsted seeing me in that light. Really, it is a hiccup in my life which is extremely aggravating. I am sure Gillian Shephard and John Major would be on my side, but I can't risk it, I daren't take the risk. And, every time something goes wrong, at the top of my voice I say; 'Gillian Shephard, where are you?'

George (Flately) found it tough keeping reception children 'on task' — a favourite phrase in the Ofsted Handbook:

> I would look at certain tasks normally and say 'Well, it doesn't matter if you deviate from that task a little bit'. I would expect them to go off and suddenly start playing around with the bottles and things, instead of making four sand castles, or planning to build a snowman instead of doing their name right. I'd expect that sort of thing, but in this environment I feel like, you're *supposed* to be doing that, I feel I have to say 'I want to see it made'. It's that constant battle all the time. The pressure is coming from the inspection.

The corporatism engendered by an Ofsted inspection does not leave room for schools and teachers to adapt their practices to the situation. It also encouraged cover-ups. Rita, a deputy head at Mixstead school, was worried that the inspection would be an opportunity for someone to damage the corporate image.

> Some are almost talking in terms of using the inspection as a vehicle to blowing the whistle on the person who's been upsetting them, and I am very frightened, that that's going to happen, because I don't want that to be levelled at the school, certainly not during an Ofsted inspection.

The fear of exposing the skeletons encourages the management of the school to develop a tight corporate approach. Schools covered up their tension points — for every institution has some — in the interests of a corporate image. In one school a particular team containing one full time worker and two job share teachers managed a superficial appearance of team work. The reality was that the two teachers did not feel happy about their job share and the full time worker had to liaise between them but

> . . . we had this agreement that we would not say anything to show that there was big division, that things had ever gone wrong at all and we didn't show one tiny crack at all. I told the headteacher 'we did this out of the collaboration to the school'.

A nursery assistant didn't feel her efforts were duly recognized by the report and she wrote a letter to the lead inspector explaining the 'invisibility of qualified nursery assistants' in general and specifically in the report. The headteacher was not keen to send it as her teacher colleague noted,

> It was like slapping her in the face when the head said, 'You don't want a whole load of HMI's to come in as a result of you saying anything do you?' So we were caught in the middle of it. We behaved very well and this is what happened to her. I feel strongly about it because it's not just personal friendship, it's that I see how hard she's worked and continues to work, how she cares about the children.

In Flately school the head teacher was asked about an obvious difference of approaches in one of his departments:

> Well, it's a shame the whole thing is a kind of contrivance isn't it? I mean to be arrogant enough to think that you can inspect a school and get the sorts of stuff that you think that we've got is just ridiculous isn't it? Because of the current way that education is set up and controlled and all the rest of it, it's in a school's interest whether they like it or not, to have a good report. So in the public sphere the importance is to have a good report, irrespective of the details, that's just irrelevant. Yes, it's a way of bringing schools to heel isn't it, to do it their way.

The problem with this form of corporateness, apart from the fact that a contrivance is reported and schools begin to work at a level of image, a symbolic existence, is that if schools cover up differences then the Ofsted team get no indication of how creatively the head and the teachers deal with differences.

A further consequence of the development of a corporate approach may well be that dominating cultures are encouraged. Letica felt that the power of a whole school culture was, ironically, preventing her from supporting HMCI,

> I've heard other people immediately jump on and criticize certain things that he [Chris Woodhead] has said that I agree with from my own experience. I don't think I'd dream of saying that anywhere apart from here, in this interview, privately.

Ironically, the pressure of corporatism may partly be the cause of a commended teacher's grades being kept secret within the school (see Amy, Chapter 2), in direct opposition to HMCI's wishes (Gardiner, 1997). The dominant approach in a corporatist culture is one of unity, sacrifice for the 'team' and the suppression of the individual (Casey, 1995).

It is the combination of national prescription, inspection and public scrutiny that encourages the governors and the head of the school to strive for a successful report. The managerialist approach that is inherent within Ofsted's Framework is a policy-led one in which each school is expected to construct a series of policies which not only conform to national criteria but which are implemented within the school in a uniform manner. It is this corporate approach that draws individual teachers into prioritizing the accumulation of a successful report over and above differentiated ways of teaching and learning.

Conclusion

Colonization is achieved through discourses as well as authoritative power. Although the Ofsted team are seen once and rarely again, the discourse of inspection and accountability remains with the schools. The Ofsted experience recedes for many teachers as time goes by, but follow up visits by LEA inspectors using the same approaches revive memories of the event and remind teachers that the Ofsted approach is the new orthodoxy. The language and discourse of Ofsted remains in terms of targets, outcomes, evidence, failing schools and teachers, and the grading system which is developed to ensure that all teachers are re-categorized as numbers. So schools and teachers remain colonized to some extent. There is 'an inner lining on the re-dressing of the school in Ofsted terms' (Field Note 10/11/95).

There are defences, appropriations and resistances, as we shall show in Chapter 5, and these temper the colonization process. Further, though we may be formed in discourses, we come into contact with a number of different, varying and sometimes contradictory discourses. Organizations themselves are multidiscursive, never a single discourse (Law, 1994). Power is not exercised all one way. Though the managerialist discourse may aim to be hegemonic, hence its unidimensionality, teachers have access to a range of discourses through which they might counteract some of the negative influences of those that assail them. This, in turn, may involve some re-positioning of themselves among these various discourses along the way (see Chapter 5). The same point applies to inspectors, as we saw in Chapter 1.

There have even been some minor modifications to the discourse under alternative pressures. For example, HMCI has outlined his assertion that all inspectorial observations of teachers should be followed up with a brief comment from the inspector (Barnard, 1997) as to the quality of the particular lesson, so breaking down those feelings of non recognition. Nevertheless the possibility that a short observation can ascertain and evaluate the complexity of a primary classroom is still in question. The consequence of continuing this form of inspection still seems to be the simplistic technicisation of primary teaching. For example, the Alexander et al. report (1992) advocated subject specialist teaching in Key Stage 1, a former minister of education called for 'paint, play and happiness' (Woods and Wenham, 1995, p. 175) to be marginalized from primary school work, and the new government's proposals to set targets for every school bring the language of technicization centre stage.

Colonization is a form of control in which many of those who are colonized accommodate the new process and the language and so the colonization creeps steadily into daily routines supported by a higher degree of school corporateness. However, colonial history shows that colonization is never total and the experience of living a colonized life actually ensures reactions against the colonizers and adaptation of the colonizing discourse. Nevertheless, primary teachers have been severely affected by this process. How they coped is the subject of Chapter 5. First, however, we must consider some of the bleaker aspects of colonization for teachers.

Notes from the Field (4)
Wednesday — The Longest Day

Day Three had been called 'dip day' by the RgI to mean a day in which teachers would feel exhausted. However, for some staff it dipped further than expected. It started OK for me as I arrived at about 3.20 in the afternoon. Evelyn was doing next term's plans in the staff room during her non contact time and she took a difficult child for a while to help another teacher who was covering a class. Asked if she had had a good day Esther replied humorously 'I got both plimsolls on the right feet.'

She then had another interview concerning her art post with the same inspector who had been difficult over the music, but there was a softer approach with which she seemed satisfied. Her earlier experience with this particular inspector was countered by Evelyn who said 'she was OK with her about language throughout the school.' It's not possible to tell how the inspectors will behave.

From 3.30 to 4.15 p.m., 10 teachers drift in and out of the staff room. On this dip day some just wanted it to end. 'I'm just getting through it, getting on with life. It was an horrendous build up and I just want to get it over and look forward to doing something else.'

At 3.43 Aileen brings up her news, 'I saw the RgI go into Tracy's room. Is everything all right?' Evelyn is sat at the table, Aileen stands with her back to the radiator thinking and Lional enters and yawns reflecting his tiredness. The phone rings and no-one answers it which is unusual. It rings again and Aileen says vehemently 'Oh God go away.' Lional tells his tale of working in someone else's class on some maths with some children and how badly it went.

At 3.45 it is noted that the RgI is talking to another teacher. A regular cover teacher — partner of one of the teachers — has had his class for the day. 'I had inspectors all day. I wish the inspector could see the children with the deputy as well as me to show how difficult they are. There was a stand up fight in PE and some children refused to do PE. It wasn't a very good today.' Esther has difficult children too. 'Isn't the weather horrible. It's so windy it's affected the children. Inspectors don't care about the weather.'

At 3.50 there are six teachers present and the depressing climate is enhanced by more stories, 'A child hit an inspector with a ball in the playground and had to write a letter of apology. The PE skills paid off then! (Ironic).' Ignoring their commitment is particularly debilitating. 'I'm pissed off. I stayed up till 3 a.m. this morning because I lost the science lesson on the computer and it was a blinding lesson and nobody came.' Other close encounters of a different nature are recounted, 'I'm glad that they didn't see my RE. I had the book on my lap as I did the lesson. A child opened the door and I jumped. I feel I don't really want to do any more tomorrow.'

She leaves the room. Letica comes in. 'The kids were horrible. My maths lesson was horrible.' Laura arrives with the only positive reactions, 'I've been a real teacher all week.' 'I haven't', says Esther depressingly, 'the music inspector has seen no evidence of appraisal or composing and that because it's not in the plans she is going to report that there is none.' The others try to help by offering examples of evidence but she doesn't write it down. Instead she rails against the process. 'I'm fed up with having to show evidence. They must see it. She wants it given to her on a plate. She won't delve into people's records.' She then remembers a family commitment 'Oh no! I forgot to phone the doctor for my son. I left him at home ill. He shouldn't be ill when we're having Ofsted.' Laura contrasts this by announcing her evening plans, 'I'm going home to make a pair of trousers', but Esther maintains her theme with more assertiveness, 'I don't want her to get away with saying there isn't any music here.' Someone else does some analysis: 'What has to be accepted in an inspection is that some lessons are better than others. I had one or two like that. Why should this week be any better?' And irony sums it up for many of them, 'Is it only 4.15? Doesn't time fly when you're having fun!'

They all leave to return to their classrooms. A visit to the Early Years department brings further depressing news. 'They didn't read my documents at all. What's the point of doing them all if they don't read them. I produced nine sheets of A4 in the holiday and she only asked about the first page.' Reports of possible fracturing relationships begin to surface, 'She asked us why the children in the nursery were so confident and average and why this was not the case in Key Stage 1. We began to feel worried that teachers in that department would feel they are being criticized if the inspector makes these comments to them about the Early Years.'

The inspectorate team ended the day by criticising two teachers in Key Stage 1 'quite unfairly' according to most of the staff. It's at this point that the 'dip day' reaches its lowest point. 'We get the dips because you put in the kicks.' 'They look smart, nice and smily but they are not.'

Two teachers, both black, were visited after school on dip day by the RgI and another inspector. Tracy was criticized for a drama lesson and told it had been marked as a failing lesson. It is unusual to see drama going on in an Ofsted inspection for it is more risky than other lessons but this particular teacher had gone ahead with it in her classroom although she usually did it in the hall but it was not available, because, 'it was good for them and I wanted the Ofsted team to see me working normally.' Her teaching is much admired by other teachers in her department: 'She's a great teacher — the bastards.'

The other teacher, Edith, was a temporary teacher in her first post. She had not been too worried by the thought of the inspection for she approved of inspections — as did Tracy. She was going to cope with inspection visits by pretending the inspector was not there. However in this particular lesson the inspector sat facing her about four yards away, 'invading my space.' People were angry with what they thought were unfair critical comments. 'She was seen eight times in three days and they only saw me five times and said nothing to me. It seems they were determined to go for the weakest link.' It was also noticed that the RgI had not conformed to the guidelines for lesson criticism as laid down by Ofsted for she had not informed these two teachers of their low gradings at the end of, either the lesson or the day on which these events occurred.

Staff gathered in support. At 5.10, six or more teachers moved from the first teacher's room to the second teacher's room to discuss the event and offer support and critique the inspectors' methods and judgments. One teacher was near to tears as she fumed at their unjust attack. At 5.20 one husband arrives to take one of them home and across the corridor the inspection team sat locked behind a closed door with their name on it 'Ofsted'.

As two of the teachers go for a cup of tea to the staff room they walk past me looking grave and don't acknowledge me. The first teacher, Tracy, slowly walks out of the school burdened by many bags and flops into her 'A' registration car and drives slowly out of the school. A few moments later the second teacher leaves, head lowered as she struggles with her bags following a few yards behind her husband who wearily fingers the car keys in his hand.

Back in the staff room people angrily comment 'it's wrong to focus on the temporary teacher. It's a waste of money.' The headteacher looks awful and has told the RgI what she thinks. She bangs the table angrily, with her fist, as she exclaims 'look what it's done to my staff. Dip day has become a self fulfilling prophecy. I'm worried now that she might resign on Friday. She's pregnant, an agency teacher, has coped with SATs and worked hard. There was no indication that anyone was going to get the knock on the door at 3.30.'

Suddenly the phone goes at 5.30. It's the first of the two teachers who wants to talk to the headteacher. I make a discreet exit and withdraw. The wind that was here on Sunday has returned if a little less strong and it is raining. Two other teachers are caught up in an altercation about something one of them said and another wants to criticize someone else for something she said to the inspector. At six o'clock we all leave. The head, the deputy and two other teachers leave, discussing how to redress the situation. It certainly has been a dip day.

Chapter 4

Feeling Deprofessionalized: The Social Construction of Teacher Emotions

The inspections themselves induced extreme emotional trauma. Stress in teaching seems an essential part of the job these days (Travers and Cooper, 1996; Woods et al., 1997), but these reactions among a high proportion of our sample were altogether unusual, and demanded explanation. Teachers' emotions have hardly figured on the research agenda as yet. This neglect is partly due to the predominance in research of what has been termed the 'cold-eyed, scientific approach' based on traditionalist middle class, male values which emphasize technicism and demote the emotions (Casey and Apple, 1989); while approaches to teaching itself have been heavily influenced by cognitive-rational models. This is particularly the case with the period following the Education Reform Act of 1988, and the institution in government policy of a market-oriented, managerialist, technical-rationalist discourse (Aspland and Brown, 1993; Hatcher, 1994). As we saw earlier, the 'Framework' that guides the approach of Ofsted inspection teams and the aims and mode of procedure of the inspectors make no allowances for emotional responses, either to the inspection process itself or to teaching and learning (Ofsted, 1993). As a result, Troman (1996, p. 32) argues, 'teaching quality has come to be defined in terms of technical competencies'. As we discussed in Chapter 2, this contrasts starkly with the strong emotional input that primary teachers make into their teaching (Elliot, 1991; Bonnett, 1994).

The emotions experienced by teachers during an inspection could not be anticipated and prepared for. For, though the inspections are scheduled through government policy, there is much about them that is unscheduled. There are no regulations or guidance by custom or tradition on how one should *feel* in such circumstances. There are no recognized procedures, formalized ceremonies, rule-governed processes on which to model one's emotional behaviour. In a real sense, teachers have to feel their own way. Even so, these feelings, we argue, are not an irrational response, a sudden and unreasonable reaction that is best controlled and suppressed, being 'simple, non-cognitive phenomena, among the bodily perturbations' (Harré, 1986, p. 2) — a view of emotions dominant since the seventeenth century. Rather, the emotional reactions of teachers to the Ofsted inspection are part of a process in which 'emotions are characterised by attitudes such as beliefs, judgements and desires, the contents of which are not natural, but are determined by the systems of cultural belief, value and moral value of particular communities' (Armon-Jones, 1986, p. 33). In this case, as we argued in Chapter 2, one system of values, the government's, which many Ofsted inspections seem to support, impacts heavily against a largely oppositional system, the teachers'. In consequence, Ofsted inspections are profoundly disturbing for many teachers. How disturbing, and with what social origins and consequences, is the subject of this chapter.

We focus on one of our primary schools to show the impact on one whole school, but also to use that school as a 'critical case' to illustrate in particularly graphic fashion a prominent line of response we have had from all the schools. In this sense it is ideal-typical. About 45 per cent of our sample of teachers were affected in this way, and reports elsewhere (for example: Haigh, 1996; Brimblecombe et al., 1995; Dean, 1995) suggest such reactions are not untypical. The staff of Trafflon consists of one male nursery teacher, six female class teachers, one female part-time teacher, a male head teacher and a male volunteer ex-teacher (full school details are on pages 6–7 in the Introduction). Two of the staff have been at the school over 20 years, and the newest is in her second year.

Having studied the teachers' emotional responses closely and experimented with a number of formulations, we argue that they are best understood as illustrations of 'deprofessionalization'. Deprofessionalization involves the loss or distillation of skills, routinization of work, the loss of conceptual, as opposed to operational, responsibilities, the replacement of holism by compartmental-ization, work and bureaucratic overload, the filling and over-filling of time and space, loss of time for reflection and for recovery from stress, the weakening of control and autonomy, and, in general, a move from professional to technician status (Apple, 1986; Densmore, 1987; Apple and Junck, 1992). Inevitably, there is a large psychological component accompanied by emotional trauma involved in such radical change. This trauma is not just a way of 'letting off steam', but serves the main social purposes of deprofessionalization. The teachers' responses show what it feels like to be deprofessionalized. At the same time, they show that their strong feelings are functional in terms of the latent aims of the Ofsted exercise, the magnitude of the change envisaged in government policy requir-ing some kind of cathartic disturbance. Seen in this way, it is necessary for teachers to be purged of their holistic sense of self and of their dedication to emotional involvement. This is inevitably painful, but beyond the pain barrier, according to this policy, lies a different, purer educational world uncomplicated by emotional responses.

In contrast to this argument, there are a number of studies that point to a measure of re-or enskilling among teachers, despite intensification (Acker, 1990; Campbell and Neill, 1994a; Evans et al., 1994; Gipps et al., 1995; Webb and Vulliamy, 1996, Cooper and McIntyre, 1996) in such areas as management, con-sultancy and collaboration, assessment, science, and the organization of teach-ing in general, with the whole business of teaching becoming more complex requiring higher levels of skill and knowledge. It might be suggested that such enskilling is taking place within a managerial discourse, but the authors above would dispute this. Gipps et al. (1995), for example, found that the majority of teachers in their sample 'did become more knowledgeable in assessment rather than being technicians operating an imposed system' (p. 176). D. Hargreaves (1994) goes as far as to suggest that the reforms are promoting a 'new professionalism'. There is pain, yes, but the debate is 'healthy' (p. 434), and there have been 'some very positive outcomes for teachers' (p. 424).

We do not seek to disprove these claims. Indeed we have noticed some re-professionalization elsewhere in our own research (Woods, 1995; Woods and Jeffrey, 1996a; Woods et al., 1997). There appear to be contrary forces at work, some enskilling, some deskilling, the outcome depending on a number of variables such as school history and ethos, experience and determination of staff, strength of local resources, amount and nature of re-training, school leadership (Ball and Bowe, 1992). All of these, of course, depend on a more general factor — the degree of negotiability in implementing policy. Ofsted inspections — some of them at least — appear to reduce the degree of negotiability, and on the showing of this case study, reveal the stark face of deprofessionalization. Whatever else was happening elsewhere in these teachers' experiences, this cast a dark shadow over them all. It continues to dim their professional worlds long after the inspection. It is an indication of what could be if this mode of approach is general, persists and is intensified. The re-skilling, in other words, as far as it exists, could be coming under serious threat.

Professional Uncertainty

The Ofsted inspection at Trafflon might be seen as a catalyst for the changes involved in deprofessionalization. Seen from within this context, it is not surprising that there should have been some confusion and disarray among the teachers concerned, and a loss of sense of reality. This was accompanied by considerable anxiety. Since existing perceptions of themselves as professionals were under attack, they began to doubt their competence and adequacy in their 'outdated' roles, and in their attempts to meet the requirements of the new ones while encumbered with the baggage of 'outmoded professionalism' — a necessary preparation for their induction into technician status. Anxieties and doubts were beginning to creep in, and normal ways of coping no longer worked. We examine each of these areas in turn.

Confusion

There was a sense of normlessness, unreality and disorientation. Corrine despairingly observed in the week before the inspection:

At the end of the day I think people will end up being less efficient. If you're asking a child 'what is 2 times 3' and they haven't a clue, you want to tackle that straight away. But you cannot deviate from your line, if you plan to stand on your head today you've got to stand on that head, that's it. I just want to pick one path depending on the problem that arises from talking to the children during the lesson.

Veronica was 'totally muddled':

Ofsted's completely there all the time now, no matter what I'm doing. I forgot to take the National Curriculum booklet home at the weekend to write down, at the side of this week's plans, exactly where it fits in and it wrecked my weekend. My other half did some ranting on Saturday morning about my reaction to forgetting them. 'They're just ordinary people and if you know what you're doing is right and you believe in what you're doing, it will be OK.' I said to him, 'You don't understand', as I sat there in floods of tears.

Cloe talked of a disappearing life:

I did 13 hours at the weekend, from Friday night right the way through to Sunday night. Sunday afternoon I burst out crying. The sun was streaming through the window; I'd been sat there since 11, and it was half past 4 in the afternoon and I had to cook the dinner and waiting for me was a pile of ironing and I just broke down and cried. It's the knowledge that your life has disappeared, you know. Beautiful afternoon and I would have loved to have gone for a walk. I'm not going to church either, because it takes up too much time.

Later on in the term just prior to the inspection, she talked in reflective terms about life after the inspection:

I'm really worried; I don't know who I'm going to be at the end of this, because I've had to come to terms with a lot of my failings in areas in which I thought I was jogging along quite nicely.

Toni had a week off for the first time in five years and on her return she talked of 'functioning without really being here'. Like her father's death, the whole process had 'taken up her life' when she felt 'the world was not really there'. Carol's car windscreen was broken a few days after the inspection, but, instead of it bothering her as it would have in the ordinary course of events, 'it was nothing compared with the inspection; I wasn't bothered'. She found it strange to be home at such an early hour in the evening. She also described how, when saying goodbye to an inspector, she didn't know whether to shake hands or not. This illustrates the confusion over some of the customary civilities of social life that attended the inspection, which exacerbated the sense of anomie. During the inspection Cloe was 'rocked' in her first engagement with the inspectors:

> It was Monday morning, quarter past 9; the children were copying up their spellings for the week and the inspector said, 'The levels of literacy are low, aren't they?' Now how would she know that at 9.15 on a Monday morning unless she's based her assumptions on the SATs results? I was on the back foot. It was 9.15 on Monday morning.

Anxiety

The headteacher, Victor, was so anxious in the week prior to the inspection, one in which Ofsted reported on 30 per cent 'poor lessons' and 15,000 'poor teachers', according to wide media coverage, that his usually affable behaviour sometimes gave way to depression. In one conversation he confessed that we had 'caught him on a downer'. He was afraid that 'the work of one weak teacher would show us all up'. Having only six classes, and only two in one Key Stage, one poor report on a lesson would clearly affect the final outcome of the report. Ofsted inspections report on achievement levels based on the yearly external SATs test results which are measured against national norms. It was clear to all the staff prior to the inspection that they would be reported as underachieving in literacy and maths because their last test results, from a total of 20 inner city children, showed this 'underachievement'. Consequently, the head and the staff feared further reporting related to 'failure', though they also believed that the school should not be designated as a 'failing school'. Clare observed:

> When the Registered Inspector talked to us for 20 minutes about the procedures for failing schools and the degrees of failure, I thought Victor was going to be carried off in a stretcher; he looked so ill.

and Carl noted that

> Victor kept saying, 'We've done so much in the last year or two' until the local inspector came round and criticized us heavily. It stopped him dead in his tracks. It was a severe body blow.

Just before the verbal report, Cloe observed that Victor 'looked terrified'. Veronica was 'sick at heart for the possible failing report' and regarded the possibility as an injustice for she was 'proud of her achievements'. Cloe was very worried about 'the emotional cost' to her and her colleagues. Clare had been told two months before the inspection that she was responsible for sorting out the special needs programme for Ofsted:

> The staff didn't realize the implications for me; they were too stressed. The day after the INSET at the beginning of the inspection term I just cried for an hour and a half, in the toilet. It was terrible, I've never done that before.

Professional Inadequacy

If deprofessionalization is to work, teachers need to feel that they have failed as professionals.

> I don't have the job satisfaction now I once had working with young kids because I feel every time I do something intuitive I just feel guilty about it. 'Is this right; am I doing this the right way; does this cover what I am suppose to be covering; should I be doing something else; should I be more structured; should I have this in place; should I have done this?' You start to query everything that you are doing — there's a kind of guilt in teaching at the moment. I don't know if that's particularly related to Ofsted but of course it's multiplied by the fact that Ofsted is coming in because you get in a panic that you won't be able to justify yourself when they finally arrive.

Feelings of inadequacy were created through what were seen as impossible targets:

> They are taking children with stable home lives, with books around them and all the things that you need for a healthy learning environment for children and they're comparing them with children who have lots of love around but the academic stimulation's just not there. They're telling us that these children are supposed to achieve exactly the same thing and that we are useless teachers because we cannot bring them up to that level because we're not on target, we're not doing our bit. It's disgusting, it's deplorable, it makes me feel sick but I'm trying not to think about it. (Carol)

However, Ofsted reminded them how far short of perfection they fell:

> However confident you are as a teacher you know that you could do better if you had more energy, if there were two of you, if you had two heads and seven arms. Because you are instrumental in the growth of these children . . . you are always going to feel a failure . . . It [Ofsted] makes you reflect, it makes you look at yourself very hard, and you

say, 'Yes, I'm not very good at that' or 'I don't do enough of that'. . . . Whatever criticism they make, it's going to feel, however stupid it is, that the last 20 years have been for nothing. It's not about what progress schools have made in the last 15 years. It's 'schools fail', 'head to be removed', 'hit team going in'. It doesn't matter what you look at, it's about failure in schools. (Cloe)

Carol argued that more professional approaches to innovation did not create these feelings:

The reason our new policy on developmental writing got off the ground was something to do with the fact that the people weren't coerced into doing things. They weren't made to feel bad about what they were doing. Instead of being told that they had got to do things that were alien to them; it was a slow, gradual process. I'm just not the kind of personality that goes around telling people what they've got to do. We've got to hold dear to that fact that forcing people into situations, being made to do things doesn't work.

Carl thought mid-career teachers were particularly affected:

These people desperately need job satisfaction. Some praise would have made them walk on air for another 12 months and they're not getting it. I think there's a psychological damage going on here that has not yet been put right. I have no hesitation in saying that they've been wounded and it hasn't been healed. It's about your worth, about your expertise, everything that they stand for has been threatened and questioned. I think it's a very serious psychological wounding. For primary teachers — I can't speak about the rest — life is very, very stressed and the one thing that keeps you going is job satisfaction, a mark or a child smiling and saying thank you and that means a hundred things.

Victor's interview with the Ofsted team left him annoyed with himself and feeling inadequate for not having exact financial figures at hand. In discussion with him after the interview it became clear that very rarely did the Ofsted inspector ask him about broad aims, which he felt was his responsibility, but about detailed figures which, he felt, was his school administrator's area of expertise. 'I told them I see myself as a leader, not as the one with all the detailed information.'

The paperwork involved in the inspection also brought feelings of worthlessness. Veronica said resignedly,

I feel now the same way as I did when I came here six years ago. I felt quite worthless as a teacher then and I feel quite worthless now. Whatever I'm doing it's not right, I can't make it fit, whatever I'm supposed to do; I can't. Whatever I do, it's not good enough.

For Carol the paperwork did not relate to her practice, as she explained exasperatedly,

> It makes me feel inadequate. I can't think like that. I can make a list of
> the things I am providing, such as Maths and imaginative play. I can
> do that quite easily, but that isn't enough. You actually have to look it
> up in the National Curriculum. It's more in depth and I find that
> completely nightmarish to deal with. There is a lot of language and
> vocabulary going on in the play corner . . . but that isn't enough anymore.
> I have to write the details of what is going on. I just can't write that down.

There was a sense of 'never finishing anything' for there was always something
more to be done on any item or issue, and more items and issues queuing up
waiting to be dealt with. This eventually affected your thought processes. Toni
was anxious, in spite of the many hours she spent on paperwork and management, that she had 'not achieved enough'.

> You stop functioning as a thinking person . . . because you end up feel-
> ing so inadequate all the time. I don't mean inadequate as in 'I feel a
> failure'. What I mean is that in the back of my mind is a long long list
> of all the things I've got to do in terms of my role: what we have done
> about our SATs results; how we have identified what we need to do to
> improve our SATs results etc. etc. etc. So until I've done it I feel inadequate
> because I haven't done it. That's the kind of inadequacy I think I mean.

Corrine, who qualified abroad, fell back on her degree as an indicator of
status, though it is not a guarantee of professional competence:

> I've got my degree in my hand, if there's any problem, I leave. When
> I was doing my degree you would die of pressure because you think
> you wouldn't pass. Why should I die now? I've got my certificate. And
> then to be made to feel inferior or inadequate, I think that's terrible;
> that's the worse thing. They tell you not to do it to children; why do
> people want to do it to you? Why do they want to say 'You're not
> good enough; you're a bad teacher; you have been labelled.' Well I
> just have to say 'Well it really doesn't bother me.' Nobody can tell me
> that because even if I'm bad, I've got the degree.

Marginalizing Positive Emotions

It would be functional for deprofessionalization if any positive emotions in
terms of teachers' own values were marginalized. Thus, energy that should be
used for teaching became side-tracked:

> Normally teachers will not use the word 'fear' and say they've been
> frightened. It's about energy and how it's used and misused and
> how it leads to sickness. Teachers are using all their energy to defend

themselves against this negative questioning. The other half of them is making sure they're giving compassion and patience and good teaching to the children, so in psychological terms inside each teacher there's a maelstrom of defence against this negative assault and making sure that none of it gets through and spoils the teaching. In psychological terms there's a terrible battle going on inside each teacher. (Carl)

The field notes show a diminution of humour, teachers' usual main coping strategy, as the inspection drew nearer, and during the inspection itself. There was some brightness on the first morning. For example, Clare was seen a number of times by the same inspector for she floated between classes, and she commented, 'You must be sick of the sight of me' to the particular inspector. But this form of humour did not last long. The head was noted for his jokes and constant loud laughter, but this fell away during the inspection. Even when he tried to joke with Clare, she cursorily dismissed it, 'I've no smiles left.' At one point the field notes (14/11/95) record a moment in the staffroom when 'Corrine was going on about her naughty children in one of the inspected lessons. There was no response from Victor. He looks very miserable.'

There was also little humour in the actual lessons themselves. Most teachers talked about how 'hard the children worked', and there were few relaxing times in the classroom. One child noted that 'Cloe was tired and frustrated and nervous. She couldn't wait to get rid of them. She was getting annoyed with us.' This contrasts with more conventional times in the classroom, for the child went on, 'She was looking sad and nervous. Normally she is humorous and teases us and jokes about her own faults and cracks jokes.'

Loss of Self

The responses discussed so far could be seen as emotional preparation for deprofessionalization. What the process centrally entails is a basic change in the teacher's sense of self. Certainly, the most telling emotional response from our teachers — literally a cry from the heart — comes from the assault on the teachers' self, for, as noted earlier, the primary teachers' self is indistinguishable from the professional role. One is fulfilled in the other. Separating them out is painful in the extreme, but again is necessary if technician status is to be achieved. These teachers' statements indicate how they felt mortified and dehumanized, how they felt they had lost their pedagogical values and holistic harmony as persons, and how, in consequence, their commitment to teaching had changed.

Mortification

For the groups that Musgrove (1977, p. 216) studied, 'The key problem of social change' was 'not competence but integrity' as Veronica exemplifies as she talked about 'the shame' she felt for capitulating to the 'Ofsted game' during the week itself after having asserted earlier, 'I won't change my practice.' Veronica illustrates here the moral issue about knowing, being and sustaining one's 'real self'. Cloe argues that it began with fear:

> I was very fearful of what it was doing to me as a person and how I would be afterwards, both in the short term and the long term. It's called into question a lot of things, I suppose; it's been a catalyst for decision-making about whether this is really what you want to be doing for the next 20 years or whatever's left and the cost. I've always been pretty tough physically. I've had a lot of things to cope with and the old body's kept going and I haven't had too many worries about illnesses but I was so run down and low beforehand. I'm still not well and it's called into question what you're doing to yourself as a human being. You start thinking to yourself, 'Why are you going through this? What are you doing to yourself? Why are you doing it to yourself?' I thought that the workload had been heavy; I had no idea just how heavy it could get. The actual inspection itself has gone but the scars it's left I feel are quite deep on a personal level.

As we saw in Chapter 3, the Ofsted process carried over into teachers' domestic lives. The emotional charge accompanied it. As a single person, Toni had to carry the emotional burden alone. She saw less of her friends, her social and aesthetic life were much reduced, and, consequently, there were times when she became depressed. Carol, who also lives alone, told stories of talking for hours on the phone to friends about Ofsted, forgetting to ask them about themselves, forgetting birthday cards, leaving parties early and hiding her favourite Jane Austen novels so she could concentrate on her school work. Veronica described graphically her life history in terms of her cruel father, the ignominies he subjected her to because of failed exams and her consequent fear of inspection and tests. Corrine told tales of breakdown in her relations with her children due to the extra work caused by the inspection, and Cloe of how she began to resent her aged mother for whom she cared. Clare talked about her husband having being redeployed and having nightmares about his intensified work, while she had to be the 'strong one' in spite of her anxiety about the Ofsted process.

The strong emotional connection between their 'selves' and their work was particularly highlighted during the Ofsted inspection, in the course of which they felt that their personal, as well as their professional, selves were being diminished.

> The whole thing was humiliating. I know that my lessons on the whole are far better than anything they saw and I found it quite humiliating that after 21 years of service in this borough, this was the first time anybody outside the school has taken any notice of what I'm actually

doing inside the school. I've had people float in and out and sort of say, 'Oh, that's very nice and goodbye', but I felt quite humiliated by the experience of having people standing in judgment over what I was doing. This sort of power, felt as though they are there to criticize. It wasn't like a teaching practice; that's a breeze in comparison. It wasn't just on what you were doing, it was how you fitted into the whole scheme of things. They stood there in judgement on me and I felt very little respect for what they could do so I found it really hard to come to terms with the fact that these people were actually judging me on my performance on a particular day. I felt degraded by it. We've talked as a staff about this feeling of being undressed by it, of being laid bare, being laid naked. It is very much a sort of professional rape if you like. I suppose they want to make you accountable and you *are* accountable for what goes on in your classroom. I don't hide away from that, but it's done in such a way as to make you feel like a victim. You are definitely their victim. (Cloe)

The cumulative effect of this assault on the teachers' self, was not unlike what Goffman (1968) has described as 'mortification' — a purging of the self that takes place in 'total institutions':

The recruit comes into the establishment with a conception of himself made possible by certain stable social arrangements in his home world. Upon entrance, he is immediately stripped of the support provided by these arrangements . . . he begins a series of abusements, degradations, humiliations, and profanations of self. His self is systematically, if often unintentionally, mortified. (p. 24)

Clare's mortification was experienced through her becoming depressed:

It took ages to get over it — an amazing amount of time — it took about six months. I was on anti-depressants from the doctor and I've never, ever, ever had that before. By Christmas, six weeks after the inspection, I was at an all time low and I had to go to the doctor. I was still bursting into tears for no reason, and the doctor said, 'you are clinically depressed' and that lasted a good 6 months. I've never in my entire life suffered from depression, ever and hope I never will again. The way I've recovered is by blanking my mind to it completely.

The school is a 'total institution' for these teachers. But whereas formerly this was a voluntary state, and one that realized and expanded the self, now it was more of a prison where their selves were to be fashioned according to the new orders. Just as an asylum for the mentally ill interrogates its patients and then makes that information the basis of its treatment, so the inspectors interrogate the teachers about the school organization and then report back to them their failures — the practice that needs 'treatment'.

Dehumanization

'Being human' is an essential part of these teachers' perception of their role. They found the Ofsted approach at variance with this. Carol felt strongly that she was like a 'slot in a machine', and then said resignedly that she 'will probably say something ridiculous' in her interview with the inspectors. Tania described the Registered Inspector as 'inhuman' and asserted that 'we're not robots', Cloe 'was fed up with being ill, not being fit enough or having enough time to be able to show concern and sympathy for others such as her aged mother and the new teacher in the next classroom'. She had taught in the school for over 20 years, travelling long distances, because she was committed to this particular school but the inspection confirmed her worst fears:

> There wasn't a feeling of 'let's move forward together, inspectors and teachers', it was a feeling of, however much they smiled their crocodile smiles and thanked you for being in your lessons (those that remembered) the fact is they were out to bite bums and they were going to bite bums come what may, because if they didn't bite bum they hadn't done their job properly.

Carol, too, had dedicated herself to the school for over 20 years. 'My family couldn't understand why I wanted to teach in the inner city,' but felt 'the stuffing had been knocked out of her and she had lost a lot of confidence'. She summed up the hopelessness for her in a slightly jocular way which nevertheless exemplified her life during the Ofsted process:

> I drive over a hill on my way home, that in the summer gives a wonderful view of Kent, and I love it. I wonder now whether I will ever see Kent again. I only ever see Sainsburys, school and home.

Victor saw it like a marathon (which he runs regularly):

> We're not at our peak during an inspection, nowhere near it, you know, it's like the last three or four miles of a marathon. You can't shout at the crowd; you can't talk to anyone; you can't do anything except go for that single minded thing you have to do. You are not at the point where you're five miles down the road where you're having chats and making jokes with people. It's just the same sort of feeling, 'I can't deal with it; I've got to deal with it; don't ask me this; don't ask me that' I think everybody's feeling that. Nobody is at their best; we're limping home.

Carl had never seen Victor in such a state:

> He was absolutely rock bottom — he was convinced he'd let the school down. He was so demoralized, he was ready to pack his job in,

literally, pack his job in. These people were reduced psychologically. It was like psychological warfare. It was a very long three and a half days. It's an emotional assault by five people who didn't deliberately set out to make an emotional assault but that's what it amounted to.

Other forms of dehumanization may be the result of laziness, inconsiderateness or worse on the part of inspectors.

And then he said to me, 'What is your name? Please spell it to me', and I spelt my name for him. If you're interviewing me, at least he should have had my name written down. Doesn't that put you off? 'S-A-B-A-H' I said to him, 'Tania Sabah'. So you're interviewing somebody and you don't know that person's name and you ask that person to spell her name for you; that is being racist.

According to Toni, Tania, now retired, had been victimized:

The end result was not what she expected it to be. . . . A lot of the staff felt very strongly that she was foolish to put herself through it and asked why didn't she retire earlier. We were all saying, 'would we spend the last year of our working life going through this crap?' but I feel the reason she did it was because she wanted to go out with an upward lift, being told you are doing so well so it would be something to leave to her family and friends. She thought an Ofsted inspection would give her confirmation of her life and work. . . . It's been a brutalizing of Tania, hasn't it? Whereas, as management we should have been gently bringing her forward and raising her awareness of what the issues were . . . rather than this execution-style finish.

A year after the Ofsted inspection some local inspectors came to do a literacy survey. Clare, a part time teacher, experienced an 'indescribable feeling':

It's as if you're not a class teacher; you don't fit into our reasoning, so you don't exist. I'm de-skilled, de-humanised. I had that all through Ofsted, who weren't interested in my plans that I'd spent hours writing. I was offering them very briefly what I felt was something positive about what they were coming to see, literacy, but they were not interested. 'No, you're not the person we need to talk to; why are you telling us?' And giving me these curious looks, and it made me feel so terrible because I'm a qualified teacher, I have to keep justifying myself to the teachers and I have something to give. I plan lessons, I teach. . . . I felt defiled. It's a strong word but that's how I felt at the end of the day as though I didn't exist . . . it was that awful lack of acknowledgment of me as a human being and of me as a teacher and me as someone of some worth. That's the feeling from the Ofsted inspection that was repeated to me last week in, Oh, so many ways.

The pressures on teachers with a managerial role to be 'managers' were undermining the human relationships among the staff that cemented the collaborative culture that was typical of the school. Thus, Toni's role as deputy head and leading curriculum coordinator led her into putting pressure on others and regretting it, even though she felt it was unavoidable. She photocopied some more statistics for coordinators to consider a week prior to the inspection, and one particular teacher, whom she liked and worked well with, reacted particularly emotively, as Toni bitterly observes:

> Tears came to her eyes, and I thought 'Oh God, I've done it again!' It's in my management role. I've got no choice. I appreciate the timing is bad but I couldn't do anything about it. I thought I was actually being quite helpful by going away at 7.30 in the morning and photocopying these bits of paper. I totally realize her reaction wasn't to do with me. It was to do with feeling very, very worried and concerned about presenting the stuff to inspectors but what I'm saying is that the end result of me trying to be helpful and efficient and giving teachers things, was to make somebody feel really, really upset and say 'I know I'm going to make a mess of this.'

The Loss of Pedagogic Values

In this particular school, there was much talk of grieving. Some of the teachers had experienced personal family grief in the recent past, and the Ofsted inspection awoke similar emotions. Also, as Nias (1993) has noted, teachers grieve for changes in practice which subvert their values. Thus, Toni felt the inspection was like a bereavement:

> I've had three close bereavements, and in particular we had to watch my father die slowly. It took up a large part of my life at the time, just like this Ofsted is doing, and at the same time it's like bereavement for I can see the old school has died.

Carol's mother, to whom she was very close, died a year prior to the week before the inspection:

> My mother died a year ago and the stress that I feel now is not the same, but it's equivalent to the pressure that I felt under. She died in September and that first term was awful for me, getting through it. . . . On my way to school I often think about things. I'm not exactly crying, but you know how you get when your eyes well up. Ofsted is like that time when my mother died; the world is not really there because you are concentrating so much on it. The pressure of visiting her and the guilt is just like Ofsted. It will be difficult getting back to reality.

She was also grieving for the loss of her pedagogy and for herself as a 'teacher as person',

> We have to be valued for ourselves otherwise there is a breakdown . . .
> All these schemes of work have taken the control of my teaching out
> of my hands. I have to fit into this. It's like a bereavement. When
> people die you feel unenthusiastic. There is a bereavement for a way of
> teaching. It is now completely out of my control. Ofsted is a realization
> of what is taking over.

Toni expressed many teachers' concerns about the way numerical analysis
was beginning to dominate their work. Her friends rang her up to ask 'if she
passed' and 'what percentage of lessons were satisfactory'. Cloe was dismayed
to find that the inspection report indicated the school was below average in
language and maths, a judgment based virtually on the SATs' results alone.
'They were like flies on dung about the figures. They were numbers to play
with.' This numerical discourse is in opposition to much of these teachers'
values which focus on people, as Veronica emphatically articulates:

> I really do feel for the children, I really do. I'm not just saying it. If you
> knew me any better, you'd know that I never tell lies. I love watching
> them succeed. But it's just going out the window.

Clare has submerged her feelings about what she feels Ofsted is doing to
working class children:

> I have blanked it out, but if ever I get into discussion with anyone, I
> get very upset. The main thing that I am very upset about is the way
> they did our children (inner city kids) down, the way that it appeared
> that our children are failing, and I know they're not. . . . That's what
> hurts me most because I've always taught this sort of kids.

Carl believes teachers are caught in a tension between holding on to their
values and suffering from lack of time and energy for their pupils:

> I became very conscious last year of the pain people bury inside
> themselves, and in the end the children lost out. (They) aren't getting
> the flowing enthusiasm that we used to see in teachers. Long-term it
> will kill the overflowing enthusiasm. Personally what kept me going
> all my career, was that I was enthusiastic. It keeps you young; it keeps
> you interested; it keeps the children excited; it's the burning fuel that
> kept me going.

Loss of Harmony

Prior to the introduction of the inspection system, the teachers felt that they
had achieved a harmonious reconciliation between conflicting elements in

their teaching role (see Woods, 1990), and between the demands of work and of their home lives. The Ofsted inspection drove wedges through this holistic perception, engendering, amongst other feelings, that of guilt. A. Hargreaves (1994, p. 143) notes that teachers are caught between 'persecutory guilt', which comes with 'accountability demands and bureaucratic controls' (see Chapter 2), and 'depressive guilt' which arises in situations where 'individuals feel they have ignored, betrayed or failed to protect the people or values that symbolize their good internal object'. 'Persecutory guilt' is clearly functional for the Ofsted mode, and 'depressive' dysfunctional. At Trafflon, there was a large amount of 'persecutory guilt' deriving from the teachers' feelings of inadequacy.

> I'm working at home on Sunday and refusing all social invitations because I want to try and achieve something and then coming home at night and working. I was very depressed and run down yesterday. I've been at Victory for six years and apart from when my father died I don't remember any other time breaking into tears but in this last academic year I've cried three times and yesterday was one of them because a member of staff upset me! Normally, I can ride things like that but it made me so angry. I just felt 'God! I'm being treated like bloody shit here!' I do everything I can, give up time to try and sort people and there's somebody having a bloody dig at me, but at the same time I felt 'Well am I losing my grip? Poor Victor, is he about to find all his female staff ready to burst into tears? Would I do that if I was a man?' (Toni)

As our teachers moved to keep pace with the demands of the inspection, they experienced a pronounced deepening of depressive guilt. Thus, Corrine felt guilty about not giving enough attention to her own children (see Chapter 3). She was born in Nigeria and was trained for secondary teaching, but wanted to know more about the English primary system her children were going through, so transferred to primary. She had grown to like it, and to become strongly associated with it personally, but the Ofsted process gradually forced apart this close relationship:

> There I am in school, telling these children to read, making sure someone reads to them, and telling them to make somebody listen to them and I'm not listening to my children. I'm so short tempered with them, you know, I don't like that part of it at all because, if you knew me you would know that I like to be happy; I like to laugh.

One of her children was admitted to hospital suffering from asthma and she felt guilty both about being late for school and for not being with her own children. After the inspection, she tried to get back earlier from school to pick them up, but when she did arrive at the childminder's they complained because they had got used to watching Sky TV and didn't want to go home. Now she is working hard to repair the damage:

I thought, during the inspection, that my children were against me as well, making life difficult for me. Now I am trying to listen to them more and trying to understand their perspectives.

The trauma of the inspection had not only affected her relationship with her children, but it had also affected her work in that she was not 'the happy person she was and liked to be'. Staff relations were also affected:

I try to be as discreet and tactful as possible in putting my message forward. I don't think Tania was ever alienated by me as a person apart from the post-Ofsted period when she was feeling victimized I said something and she snapped and it made me really upset. I don't often get that upset. She has a really bad hearing problem and instead of saying, 'Did you hear that?' I said, 'Oh, don't you remember?' and obviously it hit a nerve because she perhaps thought that I was saying that she was going senile or something, and she said, 'You can stop saying that; it really upsets me, to keep saying, "Do you remember?"'. She really barked at me. (Toni)

Teachers' feelings here reflect the conflict in modern society between dignity and honour (Berger et al., 1973). The dilemma is between being true to oneself, or to rules and regulations laid down by tradition or society. The ideal situation is where there is no conflict between the two. Musgrove (1977, p. 225), however, has written:

Personal dignity, with its basis in genuineness and authenticity, is not to be found in the performance of institutional roles which only hide or distort the real self. The lack of a sense of personal worth is no longer a private misfortune but a public injustice and legitimate base for a social movement.

Curiously, the problem in the case of our teachers is the opposite of this scenario. They had found harmony between their real selves and their institutional roles. Ofsted were uncoupling the self from the role and creating a new crisis in personal worth and public service.

Change of Commitment

In earlier work on teachers' adaptations to the government's reforms since 1988 (Woods and Jeffrey, 1996b), we noted that in spite of emotional confusion, teachers showed a sustained vocational commitment to their job. The Ofsted inspection at Trafflon put pressure on even that area. Sikes et al. (1985) have discussed how, at certain times, 'vocational' commitment can turn to 'instrumental'. Pollard et al. (1994) report a shift in this direction since the Education Reform Act of 1988 among about half of the primary teachers of their research, and this was certainly reflected among our teachers. Toni worked hard to prepare herself and the staff for the inspection after attending many courses related to planning, monitoring and record keeping, but even her enthusiasm had begun to wane:

> I don't want to lose my optimism. People always say I am optimistic but I am beginning to lose it. I don't want to be negative for I enjoy some parts, but I'm worrying about the level of support for others I can sustain as I see them suffering more and more. A friend of mine in a different profession but experiencing the same pressures is feeling the same as me. We seem to have become whingers, but that is not really who we are.

Two weeks after the inspection Carol tiredly stated that 'she felt empty and didn't want to come to school that morning'. All her ideas had been 'categorized by the inspection' and it made 'her slightly irritated. If I had the cash I'd give up and open a book shop'. Cloe expressed the feelings of many teachers in terms of work, 'I can't work any harder than I'm working at the moment; it's impossible. If it gets worse I might as well get out.' She continued,

> I think you have to prioritize your life and this has made me really focus on the fact that I have the wrong priorities. Work, career, life's too flipping short. My priorities have been too geared up towards work. I'm not willing to give any more of myself to this profession as a human being. I think they've taken enough. They've taken, I've given it freely. My emotional stability is suffering. I don't want it any more. No, it really has made me think about who I am as a person.

The intensification of the period prior to the inspection led to Toni describing herself as selfish for wanting more time to herself:

> I suppose it is selfish. I feel partly they've done that to me; they made me feel like a work horse and I now don't want to diversify and become a head teacher. I want to have more life.

She thought she was good at her job,

> but do I want to carry on doing it? I'm angry for the individual, that everybody has been sucked into getting through this ordeal, but I'm also angry with how it has pulled the rug from under my feet. From feeling reasonably okay about what I was achieving I'm left a gibbering idiot. In my heart I know that I'm doing a good job. I do, I do!

Cloe felt

> You are only seen as effective as a teacher by what you manage to put
> into children's brains so they can regurgitate in an examination situa-
> tion. Now that's not very satisfying to one's life and I reckon when the
> going gets tough, that type of person will quite happily leave it . . . My
> age group came to teaching on a tide of education for all, and all of us
> were victims in one way or another of a system that segregated the
> children at a very early age, and we saw the differences; we were part
> of those differences, and we still carry the scars. Carol and I, still say,
> 'oh we're only secondary school kids; we only went to a secondary
> modern school; we failed our 11+'. It's still having an effect on us after
> all these years. I still am worried; I haven't found me yet, not sleeping
> well. I know that I'm really wound up about these children and get-
> ting them through SATs because of the home conditions. I didn't have
> a restful break. But I don't care any more. I think that's why I haven't
> found myself because I do in fact care.
>
> I don't feel that I'm working *with* the children any more. I'm
> working *at* the children and it's not a very pleasant experience espe-
> cially when you have an over-inflated sense of importance and you
> want to take the world on your shoulders. You want to feel responsible
> for everything. You feel responsible for every part of it, whether you
> had anything to do with the test or not but at the same time there is a
> feeling of being alienated from it all, divorced from it all.

Tania, made a very specific change of commitment, retiring a year after the
inspection following a mild heart condition and time off work for stress:

> I was so confident; I was so happy; I believe in inspections; I said, 'let
> them come in and see what goes on'. He went away from the interview
> that he did with me. I didn't know if he had put down anything good.
> You couldn't read in the inspection report that it was our school if you
> covered the name up. One teacher has 'enthusiasm', another teacher
> has 'leadership', what about *me*? I'm not a piece of straw. Always I
> was praised by other teachers, by the inspectors, my headteacher is
> so happy with my work. The teachers and the parents are begging me
> to stay and I said, 'Thank you very much but I'm not staying.' I'm not
> thinking about it because I'm going to stop. If the illness was the shock
> of Ofsted I'm unhappy about it but it's made me make my decision.

We see these changes in commitment as individuals' attempts to preserve their
perceptions of their true selves. They are essentially moral actions, in keeping
with the values that drive their pedagogy. At the same time, they can be seen
as functional for the conception of the teaching profession which appears to
lie behind the process of inspection as conducted by this particular team.

Conclusion

There are other possible explanations for the teachers' reactions, especially if viewed from the perspective of the managerialist discourse. For example, could it be that these teachers were incompetent and/or inefficient, and needed reprimand and impulsion? This seems unlikely given the past record and experience of the staff, but more especially in the light of the eventual Ofsted Report, which noted 'Overall standards of achievement are broadly in line with national expectations for the ages of the pupils and broadly sound in relation to their capabilities. (para 6, p. 6) . . . The quality of education is sound overall (Ibid.). . . . Although there are gaps in some subjects, the school is meeting the requirements of the National Curriculum and RE' (para 7, p. 6). There were criticisms, for example of achievement levels in English and Mathematics, but there was no 'value-added' consideration for this school with its high proportion of disadvantaged children, so some of these criticisms are of dubious validity (see Fitz-Gibbon, 1995). Also, an average of 45 per cent of teachers in the other five schools of our research, where standards of achievement in these areas were average or above average, showed similar emotional reactions to their inspections. In general, the Report was complimentary about the staff and the school, and observed that 'the stability of the staffing contributes positively to pupils' personal development and to the continuity of care and support provided' (para 122, p. 29). Interestingly, the one teacher, Tania, who showed little emotion during the inspection was implicitly the most heavily criticized in the report. The teachers featuring in this paper were all praised. Indeed, it would seem that the more professional they were, in terms of dedication and efficiency, the more emotional they were over the inspection (Campbell and Neill, 1994a). As Carl noted:

> They are a highly conscientious staff, so the slightest criticism they are going to take personally. They are so highly involved they can't be detached. . . . Teachers need their self-esteem, their confidence boosting. I've had to go round and remind them what bloody good teachers they are. . . . They are halfway through their careers, very experienced teachers, strong personalities, know exactly what they want. They're doing all the right things, and they've been knocked off their trolleys!

Perhaps there was ineffective leadership? Again, however, the indications are otherwise. The Ofsted Report noted that 'The school is managed satisfactorily. . . . The head teacher sets the tone for the good relationships and positive ethos which exists in the school. . . . He is well supported in his role by his deputy head teacher, who has been responsible for the implementation of a range of management initiatives' (para 10, p. 7). The head teacher was criticized for 'not focusing sufficiently on the pace and scale of the curriculum development' (Ibid.), but this was in the context of general commendation. Also, it was a responsibility he had given to his deputy, so the criticism was one of judgment in re-aligning the new roles rather than incompetence. He was much respected by his staff. Clare 'loved the school, the staff and the head'. Carol admired his management style. Veronica was not too impressed with the inspectors' commendation of her work because of its dubious validity, but 'if Victor commended me, I'd respect it'. Toni, the deputy head teacher, had the highest praise for him.

Perhaps the teachers felt better about the experience after receiving the inspectors' report, their worries being a thing of the moment, similar to examination nerves? This was not the case. Weeks after the event, the teachers' perspectives of it were the same. Toni provided some respondent validation of our account:

> It [our paper] took me back to that week and the awful things that happened. In terms of the emotions it is an accurate portrayal of that week. Although I felt I was walking around like a zombie, you have picked upon the reality of it all. . . . When I read this paper, it made me feel that I wasn't having a mental breakdown after all. It shows it isn't just me. . . . The conclusion sums up what we felt as teachers. What a waste of emotion! It could have been channelled into a more positive framework.

We come back, therefore, to our argument that emotional reactions such as these are indicators of an assault on the teachers' sense of professionalism. The teachers experienced fear, anguish, anger, despair, depression, humiliation, grief and guilt — emotions produced by the mismatch between the power of the critical event they were experiencing and the cultural resources provided by their beliefs and past experiences. They showed signs of loss of confidence in the fully professional role, feelings of inadequacy, diminution of status, dehumanization, reduced autonomy, weakened commitment. In these teachers' expressive statements, we see what deprofessionalization feels like. But for these teachers, it was even worse. Their professional roles could not be detached from their 'real selves'. For them, deprofessionalization constituted an assault on the self, and its effects pervaded their whole lives. There was a measure of resistance and coping, certainly, which we will examine in Chapter 5. Overall, these strategies were to ensure a redemption of self. During the period in question, however, these strategies were overshadowed by the feelings described.

From this viewpoint the strength and pain of these emotions are a kind of rite of passage as teachers are impressed against their will from one status (professional) to another (technician). The inspection induces a trauma which penetrates to the innermost being of the teacher. In some circumstances, such trauma, as Toni noted, can be positive. Hargreaves (1983, p. 141), for example, has proposed a 'traumatic theory' of aesthetic learning, which has symptoms of

1   powerful concentration of attention and total absorption;
2   a sense of revelation and 'profound emotional disturbance', as if some part of the 'real self' has just been touched for the first time;

3 inarticulateness, as the powerful feelings drown the words, and

4 the arousal of appetite for more

But if this is positive trauma we could describe negative trauma as showing:

1 total absorption — but it is enforced, unwelcome, overpowering, and counter-productive;

2 profound emotional disturbance, certainly, but because the real self is being assaulted and damaged, not discovered;

3 heated expression rather than inarticulateness, since there is a burning need to express one's feelings; and

4 avoidance behaviour.

The inspection experienced by the teachers at this school seemed to induce such a negative trauma. Such trauma is typically produced at the liminal stage of status passages, with its critical characteristics of 'the experience of degradation, abasement and humility, a sense of reaching the limit and hitting 'rock bottom' with reality unstable and in disarray' (Musgrove, 1977, p. 223). This is one of the features of deprofessionalization — 'more like the degraded work of manual workers and less like that of autonomous professionals' (A. Hargreaves, 1994, p. 117). As Toni noted:

A friend of mine who works for a housing association told me 'I've been put on to being paid for four days but I'm still working 5 days.' I hate it [intensification] and she hates it, but we end up saying, 'I'm lucky to have a job.' Workers everywhere, it seems to me, are going through this kind of dehumanization and sense of degradation, aren't they? I have said to you it sometimes feels like we're just having a whinge, but it is wider than that isn't it? It isn't just a whinge; it's about how things are shifting in society.

These teachers had become marginalized in the no-persons' land between their own processual, child-centred, holistic philosophy, and the rational-calculative principles behind the government's reforms. Time, space, selves, preconstituted knowledge, all became problematic. But as Musgrove (1977, p. 222) points out, 'marginality may be an important prelude to deep-seated personal change'. Certainly, the teachers could be expected to seek to avoid any repetition of the trauma, as others have done with respect to assessment, where 'the publication of test scores produces feelings of shame, embarrassment, guilt and anger in teachers and the determination to do what is necessary to avoid such feelings in future' (Gipps et al., 1995, p. 173; see also Smith, 1991).

That would be one way of resolving the marginality, that is, to change, and to redefine the self. We shall discuss others in Chapter 5. The situation is fluid. The Framework that guides the inspections is being revised. Inspectors, as we have seen in Chapter 1, are not inhuman. Many schools do appear to receive 'good' reports, whatever the trauma of the process for teachers. Some research points to teachers who have found ways of working harmoniously within the National Curriculum without sacrificing their professional values (for example, Cooper and McIntyre, 1996). As time further distances the school from the inspection, and the projected four yearly cycle' of inspections succumbs to impracticability, there may then be room for the recovery of feelings of resistance and coping, and for that degree of manoeuvre that has hitherto safeguarded these teachers' values and beliefs. On the other hand, if surveillance continues or expands in this form as originally planned, on the basis of this research it could have long-term consequences for teachers' sense of professionalism and for any genuine educational improvement.

Notes from the Field (5)
Thursday — Last Performance

By Thursday lunchtime the teachers feel that they have done their stint and can see the end of this event. They raise their eyebrows to the ceiling as they pass me, 'Thank goodness there's only half a day to go. I've had enough.' Another winks at me but is looking tired and not her usual jolly self. Re-arrangements had been made in the assembly responsibilities to ensure the fit teachers fronted them. The lower school one was done by the job share teacher who works late in the week and was fresh. The enthusiastic dance teacher who is untroubled by the inspection event took the junior assembly and celebrated the raising of £2000 for charity by another teacher in the marathon.

Time dragged during the whole week. A support worker noticed how time normally flies during the week but this particular week didn't, 'It's only Thursday.' Events which exhibit tension and crisis slow the passage of time and ensure a longer focus on the stressful experiences of the people involved. Even her commitment is beyond the call of duty, 'My dad is in hospital but I came in all week because it was Ofsted week.' She noted the uniformity: 'They all dress the same, with only slightly different straight smart skirts and dark suits'.

Resistances to orders were more in evidence: 'She wanted to see me now but I said "No, 12.30. I need a break".' 'We should ignore the report for we have no respect for their judgments.' Tiredness affected everyone. Even the trousers didn't get made: 'I slept from 9.30 p.m. to 6 a.m.', 'I usually read at night but I haven't done for three weeks'. The event is all consuming. The part-timers who came in later in the week were not excused anxiety for information about the engagements were passed down the line, 'I had a panic attack at 9 o'clock last night after talking to Linda over the phone. I went and talked to a RgI who lives next door.'

Others continued their survival strategies by eating vast amounts of chips, 'I've never eaten so much rubbish food in my life.' One of the teachers, criticized the previous evening by the RgI, eats her dinner quietly on her own at one end of the room, though after a while Aileen goes and talks to her. The head reports that two inspectors and the RgI are with the other teacher, Edith, and then she says that she felt quite nervous at the podium in her assembly. There's some laughter about the lectern and how she didn't use it. Letica, who showed some anxiety prior to the event recounts the terrible atmosphere of yesterday and says she is relieved it wasn't her who was criticized and that she feels sympathy for her friends and colleagues in what she feels was an unfair incident. For a while the chat turns to the children and then away from the children and then one of them spots me and accuses me of bringing them back to the event by being there.

A few of them then discuss the details of the observation of the temporary teacher by a particular inspector, the invasion of the teacher's space and the inspector is ridiculed. The sympathetic teacher gives evidence that she has only been seen teaching groups and not in front of the whole class. Where there is humour it is concerned with the difference in power positions. 'I've sat outside the head's room waiting for interviews with the inspectors so many times this week it's like being back at school as a pupil.'

At this point the teacher criticized for her drama lesson comes in and sits at the main centre table. She says 'It was the management of my drama lesson they criticised. I've had my ups and downs. I'm OK now' she bravely asserts. The tone is changed quickly by the deputy head who is at pains to recognize how good the children have been during the week and stories are told of children performing brilliantly during questioning from the inspectors. However, this doesn't last long. 'Only two and half hours and then they can just bugger off.' Tracy comes in again, near to tears, as she tells the story of how the RgI and another inspector came to see her at 12 p.m. for a further interview. She told them that her interview was timed for 12.15 and they confirmed the time as 12.00 for 'an interview with Mrs —'. '"That is not me" I said, and they apologised and went off to see the other black teacher. They probably can't tell us apart.'

Two teachers report that they have not been seen teaching language and a teacher is critical of an inspector asking a child 'what wars took place in Tudor times?' The temporary teacher, Edith, explains that she held her own in her conversation with them this morning as she explained her version of the events the previous day and how she had forgotten to put helpful words on the blackboard for she had been nervous. Another teacher describes her bad lesson, 'It was going badly and instead of sorting it out I sunk under it and carried on thinking "I don't want to be here." Do you really need someone to tell you it was a bad lesson?' and then recounts feelings of irritation, 'I wondered why I was pleased with an inspector telling me I have some good strategies to deal with stroppy kids. I felt resentful and wondered why on earth I was feeling pleased about it. I should have said "I know I have. I've been teaching for 25 years".'

This explosion of resentment concerning her professional competence and the demonstration of power differentials was immediately mingled with a more mundane tale indicating the effect of Ofsted inspections, 'I lost my car keys on the first morning of the inspection and haven't found them since.' By this time everyone had drifted back to their classrooms for the last time.

During this last afternoon evaluations were taking place in the staff room. The head observed 'I'm amazed at what they haven't read.' Another teacher observed 'How little they know of our work. They seem obligated to check on certain things and so do so with a cursory look.' Others reported, for the last time, about close encounters, 'Thank goodness she left just before I couldn't find my geography worksheets' and others of more positive encounters, 'The report back on the science was good as was the PE.' Others ignored it at breaktime and talked about football and conversely the part time teacher described the 'lesson from hell. I made sure I wasn't nervous. I was my usual jolly self and had a chat on the carpet with the children but they were awful.' These varied stories were becoming normal staff conversation with hardly a comment made. One teacher who was not adversely affected by the whole event phoned a florist for flowers for the head and deputy head to be presented at a celebration on the following day and another teacher talked to me for a while and said it was good to have someone to chat to about it all.

After the end of the school day, most people drifted into the staffroom and plans about the future took over from stories about the inspection. 'When I told my son it was the last day he said, "does that mean you will talk to us tonight?"' She outlined her plans, 'I'm going to have a good story with my kids tonight even though the house is a tip. I didn't do my timetable for the last lesson. It was a great feeling, really naughty.'

However, the day was not over yet. Some tales of the event were still to unfold and some were still being enacted. The teacher criticized for her drama lesson sat wringing her hands and wiping her forehead and cheeks and hanging onto her coffee cup tightly. 'I woke up at 2 a.m. and couldn't get back to sleep with things turning round in my head. Things were buzzing around, "How am I going to approach today? What am I going to say to them?"' and the other teacher involved said 'It was the same for me.'

Nevertheless, they also recognized that this was a nervous time for the head and deputy 'having to wait for feedback'. More positive feedback was intermingled with these stories, 'the PE and the SEN was great. Give yourselves a pat on the back. Have I got to do a dance?' to which the reply was 'Oh no, I'm too tired to watch.' More feedback ensued with people going round the table reporting mostly in a quiet manner. The 'dancer' reported to me that, 'I consider this a positive experience, absolutely fabulous and I didn't feel any different in the classroom than on an ordinary day.' For one teacher at least the engagement was an invigorating and highly positive event.

There were general themes running through all reports concerning the curriculum subjects, 'more monitoring and more assessment,' which became the touchstone for humour as it was repeated with each report. Another theme was 'they didn't tell us anything we didn't know' implying the futility of it all. The consequences of 'presentation of front' are examined and the judgments then assessed as hollow, 'After ten years I'm told I'm good at discipline. It makes me feel like shit because the whole inspection has made the kids act well anyway,' 'It's not real,' 'It's bad for your health.' 'What have we learned — to cope under pressure.' 'Our standards are all right but we knew that. It has only confirmed it.' 'I've learned I'm as big a show off as I thought I was.'

Slowly, from about 4.45 half the staff leave, some with very different feelings from the last few months, 'Do you notice anything. I'm not carrying anything.' This is contrasted with behaviour the previous night, 'I was obnoxi-ous last night at home. I snapped at them all. They left me in the kitchen saying 'we've done this and that for you and you behave like this.'

Gradually they leave until a hard core of 10 people are left. They ruminate over the part played by politics in Ofsted inspections and the high levels of teacher demoralization due to the critical public focus on their work and they try to come to terms with the end of an overwhelming event, 'I feel I should be doing something. I've been so long doing things.' I leave them to their feed-back from the RgI but on the way out pick up a rumour that two teachers have been given excellent teacher gradings. The event is not over for all of them.

Chapter 5

Coping with Ofsted Inspections

So far we have portrayed teachers as being very much on the defensive. Their time and space have been colonized, their sense of reality disturbed, and they have experienced feelings of deprofessionalization. But 'all strategies of control call forth counter-strategies on the part of subordinates' (Giddens, 1985), and teachers are very resilient. In previous studies we have remarked on their powers of adaptation and resistance (Woods, 1995; Woods and Jeffrey, 1996b). To some extent, this reaction has been facilitated by the 'implementation gap', as was the inspectors' implementation of the inspection as discussed in Chapter 1. Part of the rationale in establishing Ofsted was to decrease this gap, to ensure that government policy was being carried out in schools, and to close down resistance. This is a comparatively new kind of constraint on teachers. In the past, they have had to cope with more 'neutral' factors that have become almost part of their jobs, such as state of school buildings, class size, salary levels, or recalcitrant pupils. As is shown in Chapter 2, Ofsted represents a direct intervention from above in a hierarchical system, operated by strangers employing a discourse foreign to most primary teachers. These circumstances are not new to most teachers but as we have shown in preceding chapters they profoundly affect the teachers and to some considerable extent dominate their lives. So how do teachers cope with this new constraint?

We found teacher responses here to be complex, and in some respects contradictory. At the same time as they were experiencing colonization and deprofessionalization the teachers were developing coping strategies. The latter in themselves contained apparently contrary behaviours. On the one hand, teachers *distanced* themselves from the Ofsted process in order to maintain their selves and professional identity. At the same time, they *engaged* extensively with the process in order to satisfy the corporate pressures and their faith and commitment to work. These behaviours were generally exhibited simultaneously by the majority of the teachers although within these categories teachers positioned themselves differently.

Distancing

Teachers developed various forms of role distancing together with some withdrawal from the process. These strategies were reinforced by social solidarity, characterized by a large degree of humour.

Role Distancing

The radical reforms of the late 1980s and early 1990s have brought about a new official conception of the 'good teacher' (Troman, 1996; Woods et al., 1997), which the Ofsted process endorses. The emphasis has moved from the predominant 'personal qualities' of teachers prior to the introduction of the Education Reform Act of 1988 to a tightly specified set of competencies, with the most significant change being that from 'teacher' to 'teacher manager'. Our teachers were keen to maintain their own identity as a teacher, so, to some extent, they distanced themselves from the official conception. This is not an outright rejection of the role, for this kind of distancing was like that described by Goffman (1961, p. 95), where the individual denies 'not the role but the virtual self that is implied in the role for all accepting performers' (see also Snow and Anderson, 1987). In contrast to the managerialism with which they were confronted, teachers contributed to what we have termed elsewhere a 'new professional discourse' (Woods and Jeffrey, 1996a). We identified six features of that discourse in the Ofsted process.

The Affirmation of Valued Pedagogies

Georgina (Trafflon) asserted, 'We go from where the child is. We ask where these children are; that's where we start. The inspector is obviously feeling that we ought to pitch our curriculum at the level we think the children should be and only if they don't cope should we differentiate.' Frank (Cottingly) argued that the lack of spontaneity was reducing creativity:

> There used to be time to talk. I can remember lunch times; you'd have a game of chess, which I thought was terribly important. Taking risks is important. When children bring things in which are not necessarily to do with what you've got to do there used to be time to go off the rails. I'd hate to see it all narrowed down. My horror would be that everybody in the country at 10 o'clock does fractions.

The Analysis of the Political Process of the Market Philosophy

The inspection report on Flately school was publicized by the Local Education Authority, local media and local television as a 'good' report', but Robina observed that

> the government's plans have worked to create this atmosphere where schools would have to compete against each other. Heads of other schools are using it with their staff in preparation for their Ofsted exam saying 'This is an inner city school, we can do it'. Schools, parents and everybody are now going to be sold the story that Ofsted is OK.

The Use of Comparative Material to Put the Event into a Wider Perspective

Otterley (Mixstead) was 'quite severely affected a week before we came back'. One of her son's friends, an 18 year old, was killed in a car crash a week after 'A' Level results. 'It puts life into perspective for you, you know; Ofsted can't be worse than this sort of thing'. Toni (Trafflon) enhanced her perspective by engaging with papers written by the researchers, and read by her for respondent validation. 'I found it useful in that it became clear that other people were experiencing similar things. It was just confirming I suppose for me how bad it was because you were writing it as an outsider . . . you picked up on the reality of it all.'

Expanding One's 'Reference Set'

This was done, for example, through attachment to other institutions and activities (see Nias, 1989, pp. 204–5). One headteacher's mother had a 90th birthday some 200 miles away on the Saturday prior to the inspection but she decided it had to go ahead, 'Ofsted is not the big thing in my life until Sunday night. I am going to spend a little time sorting out my assembly for Monday but most of my focus is on my mother's birthday.' Katherine (Mixstead), at the other end of the scale was focusing on the problems of getting engaged. 'This is my biggest concern at the moment! But that is the struggle I think that everybody has. Your personal life doesn't stop just because of Ofsted.' Georgina's (Flatly) Ofsted coincided with moving house and she had two young children that helped keep the event distant from her, 'I'm sure that if I had more time I would give more time but I go home and I have two children who want my attention and you forget school. You can't be thinking of everything.' Leila, at the same school, also felt that her own children gave her another perspective on life but she still found herself telling them 'not to be sick during Ofsted week. What a terrible thing for a mother to say.' After an inspection however, teachers turned back to their families. Amy (Lowstate) was determined to recover her relations with her own children. 'We've made special arrangements for Friday night to get a pizza delivered and we're having a video all together, and they're going to have Tango and I'm going to have a bottle of red wine! They don't even want to go and see the fireworks. They just want to stay in with me and we're just going to keep saying, 'We can have a life instead of Ofsted.'

Sherina and a few colleagues at Flatly were determined to carry on with a yoga class in the school during the week itself even though they 'wondered whether they would think us odd'. In the event they were 'too exhausted to do it'. Lional (Lowstate) used physical means to distance himself from the event itself. 'During the week I did quite a lot of physical stuff, quite a few long walks across the downs and that was good. I'd decided beforehand that I was going to make sure that I got physically tired so that I would sleep and recover.' Carol (Trafflon) school signed up for a course soon after the inspection and tried to escape from the low point at which it had left her, 'Last week we had Harold Rosen speaking to us and he was fantastic. We could really do with somebody coming in, firing us up and making us feel good about ourselves again', whereas Clare (Trafflon) used Christmas to distance it. 'I'm not thinking about it any more, I am channelling myself into giving these children a great Christmas.' To bolster rhetorical distancing and the attachment to other institutions they created their own images and they embarked on procedural criticisms to invalidate the examination.

Creating Mythical Monsters of the Ofsted Team Through a Kind of Contrastive Rhetoric

The teachers used stories from other schools and friends and folded these into their own events. Frederica (Cottingly) related how the teachers in another school 'were in school all over Christmas. On the first day of the inspection one teacher resigned, and since the inspection three teachers have been on sick leave and one staff member is up in front of the head for incompetence'. Esther (Lowstate) recounted how one of her colleagues knew of an Ofsted inspector who gave up the job when she was asked by a little boy 'Why do you make my teacher cry so much?' Shula (Flately) asserted that teachers were, in spite of an Ofsted Framework, 'driven by what we don't know and to keep a unified personality we have to see the inspectors as bogies'. Amy (Lowstate) created a mythical inspector called Fred, 'The children come up to me and say, "Would Fred be pleased with that?" It wasn't an intimidating Fred; it was just like my mate'. Toni, (Trafflon) meant to keep a scrap book of everything going on with Ofsted so she could maintain her own distance. 'I wanted this scrapbook of how bloody awful it was. The irony is that I've never had the time to cut the bits out and stick them in a book!'

Procedural Criticism

The teachers made critical comments about how the inspection was conducted, based on their own professional knowledge and experience (see Sandbrook, 1996). Francis (Cottingly) claimed that inspectors 'made a lot of judgments which were unfounded because they hadn't checked their facts. That's what annoyed me — that they were making sweeping judgments without actually having a complete picture'. Lional (Lowstate) saw Ofsted as only one perspective amongst others. 'They're entitled to their point of view but we know very well that some things written there aren't quite accurate and so in that respect we don't need to see it as the only analysis of our school.' Their approach to eliciting information from pupils was seen as inappropriate:

> Whoever walks into my room is treated as a guest in the classroom and they were treating it as though it was their damn right to do what they liked and to upset any lesson. He went round and fired questions

at the six children whose work I had been asked to select and I was absolutely horrified. I wouldn't do that to children, OK. (Cloe — Trafflon)

Kay (Mixstead) found it 'difficult to accept their criticisms of maths in the school when I didn't personally have anybody come in when I was doing maths'. Kieran, at the same school, noted that, 'apparently he saw seven music lessons in Key Stage 2 and I know that four of these lessons were in the year 3. So you get a distorted picture, and then there were criticisms made of year 6's music, but he hadn't been in there at all'. Rose was concerned about reliability. She had been commended in her school's inspection but if she were in a school where there was an inspection due . . . 'I still have this strong feeling that I could still get the thumbs down. It's people's personal opinion.' This turned out to be prophetic for when a local inspector came to do an inspection six months later her curriculum content and approach was criticized.

Withdrawal

If all else failed, an extreme form of distancing was withdrawal (Woods, 1979). Of over 80 teachers involved in the research covering six schools only one absented herself from the process. Naomi's (Morghouse) mother died some three weeks prior to the inspection and although she attempted to return to work just prior to the inspection she found that the need to grieve for the death of her mother superseded the pressure from the school management to turn in for the Ofsted inspection itself. 'There are more important things than Ofsted, like birth, love and death.'

Francis (Cottingly), an ex-college lecturer, ensured her corporate duties were kept to the minimum and then focused on her priority which was the education of her year 6 pupils in their last term at the school. 'I'm not resisting it; I'm just not accepting it at the moment, because there is enough pressure elsewhere.' Her past status and her competence in the school's eyes appeared to inure her from the corporate pressures. However, this form of practical withdrawal was not seen in any of the other schools.

Three teachers retired within a year of their inspection, though none had planned to do so before. Tania (Trafflon) near retirement, absented herself a few weeks after the report was published which she felt was critical of her. The official reason for absence was a heart problem, 'it was the shock from the Ofsted and so I'm unhappy about it and that made me make my decision'. For Frank (Cottingly), aged 63, it was 'all the interference from the government and outside bodies, so I thought I'd go now rather than wait for another two years because I could see things getting worse. So much of the pleasure is going from it'.

There was also a certain amount of tactical withdrawal. After the inspection, following criticisms of their SATs results, Cloe (Trafflon) resolved to do what they wanted, 'Well if that's what they want, bugger it, do your time and get out, you know, there's no point having any ideas.' Clare (Trafflon) withdrew from the staffroom 'as they came in, I came out — I really could not stand it. I haven't recovered in the sense that I've talked it through to the very end because I don't feel better about it. It's still raw for me and seeing the local inspector, a year later, acting in an Ofsted manner makes me realize that now'.

Solidarity

The reconstituting of the discourse was strengthened by doing it together (Woods and Jeffrey, 1996a). The inspection bonded teachers in a school in terms of coping (although it separated them in terms of colonization, as discussed in Chapter 3) such as to produce a certain communitas (Turner, 1974). There is 'a strong feeling of camaraderie, a sense of common destiny, mutual support, the absence of stratification by age, ability, social class, gender or race, the transcendence of status and role as they apply to normal life, and great excitement and enthusiasm' (Woods, 1995, p. 93). Communitas is usually witnessed as a direct result of one's own positive actions (as in Woods, 1993). Here, it developed in response to a perceived threat. Nonetheless it showed some of the same characteristics. For example, there was a great feeling of collegiality and mutual support. Carl (Trafflon) noted, 'I'm old enough to remember the war where everybody pulled together. All this classroom work has been like 1941; everybody wanted a go.' When Frances (Cottingly) apologized for missing the staff meeting at 8.30 on the first morning of the inspection 'the head put her arm round her and hugged her' (Field Note 3/7/95). Enid (Mixstead) volunteered to do a class assembly during Ofsted week. These performances were considered by all the schools as important examples of their work:

> In the long run, I've put a bit extra into this particular assembly. It is probably what I would have done anyway, but you are just more conscious . . . You always want them to do their best, but if anything goes wrong well then it is not the end of the world, but this time I'll try and make sure that they know it. The staff have given me their hall times this afternoon, and they've helped with the costumes. If I ask they do help me. If you look around and there is nobody there, and they have all gone home or something, you think; 'Blow it, I won't do it again.' I don't mind doing things if they support me.

The heads were found to be round the school more often, providing extra support and offering help with displays, as Rachael (Mixstead) shows:

> I said I would do the drama studios, so that they could see that I could do something practical as well, and so that I can turn around and say; 'Right. I have told you your room looks good, now get down to my

library and feedback to me the improvement. Say something about the drama studios, the posters that we put up.' So I am trying to say that we are in this together, without me treading on their toes.

Helen (Cottingly) talked about a holiday to Ireland during half term and how she felt she had to apologize for not coming into school as everyone else did. The staff supported her and discussed why she should feel so defensive as to have to apologize for not coming in. However, teachers were also often determined not to discuss the inspection as they socialized. Lional (Lowstate) observed, 'There are certain times when talk about Ofsted inspections is taboo.' They went to the theatre together, and a couple of schools continued with the school play, which took their minds off Ofsted. In Cottingly,

> There's always at least one reference to a play or a film when I've been in here. Perhaps that's one of the ways in which they manage to resist the pressure of school and Ofsted and there's a group of them that do go to these arty things. (Field Note 14/6/96)

This group of teachers always entered the parents yearly 'Trivia Quiz', and this year was no exception, even if it was a couple of weeks prior to the inspection.

On the Friday night at about 6 p.m. prior to the Monday inspection Aileen (Lowstate) was still worrying about how to organize the three children's trays that were to be inspected. They contained at least 15 folders and another dozen books. 'It's not because it represents who you are but if all else fails, this will be my proof; this is my evidence.' Aileen was nearly in tears because one book which recorded a child's reading over the year was missing and she went to the Secretary's office to telephone the child's home but was eventually persuaded not to do so by a group of teachers who had congregated around Aileen's room:

> The headteacher, Letica, Angelina and Esther carried Aileen's trays ceremoniously across the playground to the inspectors' room, joking about losing some of these folders or books. When they returned with Aileen, with tears in her eyes, Angelina, the deputy head, put her arm round her shoulder and told her that she'd done everything possible. (Field Note 17/5/96)

Aileen remarked later, 'The positive aspects are that it pulls the team together; people are rooting for each other and want everyone to do well, and when you've had a bad day people are concerned for you. It's normal in lots of ways though not to the same extent as now and Ofsted crystallizes that.'

Others were brought into the support group. Erica (Mixstead) had a bad second day and this affected her whole inspection. The week after the inspection all her family arrived from the north for the weekend. 'They hadn't been here for 26 years. My mother knew me and how it affected me. I talked to them about it.' Aileen's (Lowstate) father arrived from Scotland for a week or two prior to the inspection to cook and help out with such things as sharpening pencils and her husband took charge of the cooking. Toni (Trafflon), a single person, appreciated her mother's efforts: 'I went home last night and found that my mother had come round in the middle of the day and just put some soup in my fridge for me; my sister is making computer labels for me. She comes into school after her work as a nurse.' Another headteacher who was on the governing body at Cottingly came in one Sunday morning to help and was assigned to tidying up the stock room. One husband came and stood at the school gates one afternoon to watch an event involving his wife's invitation for a fire engine to play a part in her curriculum during Ofsted week. She was anxious about whether she may have taken too much of a risk. 'It was good to know that he was just standing there although I couldn't see him' (Kay — Mixstead).

Pupils also rallied round. One child brought Bronwyn (Cottingly) her stress ball, a little spongy thing that you squeeze. 'I thought you might need that' she said. One year 5 boy postponed his hospital appointment unbeknown to his parents to be there to help his teacher. Even the researchers were drawn into the support process. Rosa told Bob, 'You have got a soporific type voice you know, like Peter Rabbit. It has a soporific effect on you. You are going around being calm and relaxing just like the story.' Cloe (Trafflon) also appreciated the researcher's presence: 'I've got an elderly mother and I can't talk about anything to do with school to her, so I can't off-load there; your friends get fed up with hearing it, so it's rather nice to have this impartial ear.'

Parents similarly were supportive, and the simple central message of one report promoted solidarity with the community because of the school's context.

> One parent appreciated the 'good report', saying 'thank God for that; isn't that wonderful, that somebody is saying something positive about this area, for once' . . . She was talking about 'parents holding parties, and the tenants' association should be making a big thing about this, to celebrate these positive comments about our area, because it's *our* school and therefore it's our area. So, it wasn't just for the school, it was for the whole community'. (Field Note 2/4/95)

Humour

Humour was the cement that held the solidarity together. McLaren (1986, p. 163) talks of a 'culture of pain' that students experience at school against which they raise 'a laughter of resistance'. Teachers have also been experiencing a 'culture of pain' bringing stress levels among teachers to record heights (Woods et al., 1997). 'The cries, the gabbled stories, the exaggerated gestures, and the loud collective laughter dominated the staff room on the Friday after school in the staff room' (Field Note, 3/7/95). To some extent they, too, employ a 'laughter of resistance' both to distance themselves from, or to reconstitute, the managerialist discourse and to boost their morale. Glen described it as 'Battle of Britain' humour. Laughter offers a way of 'redefining power structures' and reclaiming a sense of collective identity (McLaren, 1986, p. 161; see also Mealyea, 1989). It is a way of making alliances (Bradney, 1957; Coser, 1958; Emerson, 1969), of drawing other like minded individuals into the struggle, and cementing them within the discourse. In this sense, humour is power. The following forms were prominent.

Exaggerated Metaphor

The force of the humour lay in the graphic and intense nature of the comparison, together with its own humorous connotations. Grace (Flately) thought the experience of an inspection could be seen like the sex act, 'lots of activity and noise and afterwards we're not fit to do anything else'. She asserted that 'you'll need an elephant stun gun to slow me down. The tranquillizers are not working' and that due to 'the hot flushes I've taken off my thermal vest'. Gloria, at the same school, thought it was like ballroom dancing when you're doing a performance: 'you don't want to do a wrong step'. Raymond (Flately) thought it was like 'the Alamo, the night before the attack with people all in their own rooms writing letters home'. Freda (Cottingly) allowed the researcher to step in and take her class to give her a break: 'I can just see it in the book — "teacher goes loopy with stress".' Leila (Flately) reflected 'I haven't thought what I'm going to do after the inspection except expel air.' Tania (Trafflon) likened the preparation to slavery: 'It shouldn't be such hard work. We have to have some inspections but it is so hard. We're like the pyramid slaves with aching arms, necks and backs. However, *they* left behind something substantial'.

Joking

Goffman has observed that joking is a way in which the individual makes a plea for disqualifying some of the expressive features of the situation as sources of definition of one's self; and to participate with a group of one's similars in this kind of activity can lend strength to the show of role distance and to one's willingness to express it. Frank (Cottingly) used jokes to good effect to maintain a good school atmosphere. 'Which art medium are we going to use in this term's art plans? — Large ones.' 'We have been told we must not put "finishing time" on our timetables so let's call it "Extended studies"' (Field Note 14/6/97). His staff used him as a butt of humour when he mildly complained about extra work while the head was away on a school journey, and the staff started singing 'When it's 6 o'clock their mummies and daddies will take them home to bed because they're tired little teddy bears'. Tony, a supply teacher at Flately volunteered to help, 'I'm taking all the worry off the rest of you teachers, by not working this weekend' (Field Note 4/2/95). His headteacher kept up the banter by announcing after the inspection that 'The only one who failed is you Tony.' Cloe (Trafflon) was so busy that she decided to 'write with the right hand and eat with the left'. Even the researcher was brought into the joking,

'Jenny looked at me writing notes and said in a loud voice "I'm going to the loo for the first time this morning. Bob's going to write that down".' (Field Note 4/2/95)

Ridicule

This is a more direct assault on the opposition, cutting them down to size and neutralizing the threat. There was amusement in the Flately staffroom at the new 'prayers' introduced which were called 'reflections'. The staff at Trafflon made up an acronym for Ofsted: 'Old Farts Studying Teachers Educating Diversely', and they paraded the newspaper cartoons about 'Oftos' (Bell, 13/11/95) next to their inspection timetables on the staffroom board. Bronwyn (Cottingly) expressed the hope that 'they come into my PE to see my new plimsolls that cost a fortune'. Francis (Cottingly) had not only 'not filled in the form but I've forgotten what it was for', and had 'lost her lie sheet, you know, the timetable'. Cloe (Flately) was going to 'remove my watch when this is all over', and Neville (Morghouse) was gratified to receive a commendation about his maths expertise when 'I had only read it up the night before.' One head ridiculed the inspection on the first day but at the same time got over his messages:

> The head and the senior management team arrive in the staffroom. He's got an armful of folders with papers in and he starts by demanding that a comment is re-written on the staff room notice board, 'someone's rubbed it' out he says. 'Off day number one. Put it up, put it up. Off day number one'. There's a slight pause. A few people laugh; they know what he's alluding to. He then shows them a folder and describes what's inside it. 'There's one for everybody here' he says, 'there's a register of the children in your class just in case you've forgotten. . . . there's some science records in here', and there's a laugh from other members of the staff management team who admit they've only just done them. He says, 'there's the names of the inspectors and the subject they're inspecting' and someone calls out 'Oh and their star signs I hope'. There's laughter and he says 'there's another chart here which tells you which day they're in school and then he says ironically 'if you were hoping to see Mr Elms for maths, I'm afraid I must disappoint you, he's not in today'. Again lots of laughter. And then he says 'there's a list of what they're looking at, thing like punctuality'. It's a half joke and people laugh and then he says smilingly 'well actually punctuality is quite important, make sure you get out into the playground on time with the kids and all that crap' (Field Note 6/2/95).

Self Parody

This is another technique to bring the whole process to earth and to put it in the plane of the ordinary, in this case through joking about one's own fallibility.

Aileen has the staff in fits as she explains how while rushing to leave home for the inspection her husband asked 'Why are you putting on two bras?' The staff at Cottingly parody themselves talking to the children: 'You could do it if you tried just a weeny teeny little bit harder', and Shona (Flately) explains graphically how she gritted her teeth and replied gently and supportively to a pupil who knowingly had suggested that 'light travels by bus' in answer to a question. In more bitter circumstances, Helen (Cottingly), after getting a critical report about art, laughingly asks for help in the staff room over a lesson 'for we are no good at art in our department'. A month after the inspection Raymond read out his report to his staff:

> 'We have to get 91 per cent or above with attendance or we have to comment on it, so we fiddled it.' The question of whether these comments he makes are true or not is in dispute but he does this self deprecating, slightly cynical approach which is very much part of his management style. He says 'I'll start now and if you get bored throw something. I'll explain some of the words so "follow with your finger."' When he comes to a part where it talks about 'all the children achieved equally', he says 'we're obviously a bit cliquey about who we teach'. Again laughter. A comment in the report describes the consultation on the school development plan as being good and he looks up and says, 'is it?' and there's a laugh. The priorities in the school development plan were said to be 'constructed well' and he remarks, 'and never to be seen again'. A following comment in the report goes on to say that the school development plan helped in raising achievement, 'Blimey!' he says, indicating what everyone knew, that the SDP had been cobbled together beforehand and certainly couldn't have been the cause. There was a loud laugh at this. (Field Note 24/3/95)

Collusive Humour

Humour is a good vehicle for breaking down institutional roles (Goffman, 1961). There were attempts to reach across the structural divide and make contact with the inspection on a human level. Grace (Flately) recounted how she was determined to 'break down this woman'. She used humour by talking in defensive tones to her children about her Skoda car and was pleased to see the inspector begin to laugh. During a department meeting, she winked at her team and talked of having two more meetings the following week while an inspector was observing, which they all realized was a joke. Georgina could not contain her laughter and had to leave the room under the pretence of using the photocopier. It became common knowledge that Grace had had no visits for the first two days and one of the inspectors colluded with her: 'I bet you thought I was coming in at last but I'm not.' On the other hand, Gloria (Flately), who had had a lot of visits, suggested, 'Why don't you share yourselves out; some teachers are getting quite lonely.' When her PE lesson began to become unruly at the end of the day she smiled at the inspector and said 'They're very tired', and he nodded in sympathy. Clare (Trafflon), who floated and encountered one inspector a number of times said 'We really must stop meeting like this'. One RgI began his introduction on the morning of the inspection in the staff room with a pretend grab for the biscuits to lighten the tension. Another inspector was present when Bronwyn (Cottingly) began an RE lesson with a story that the children said they had heard the previous week and he 'teased me four times during the week about it'.

As we have argued before with respect to pupils,

> because humour allows the expression of conflict in socially accept-able ways, it is acting also in these instances as a coping agency. It is meeting constraints, problems, contradictions and so forth in a per-sonally creative way that allows for the preservation of selves and for a modicum of social order to be maintained. (Woods, 1990, p. 208)

Engagement

Teachers could not avoid the event. On the contrary, it imposed itself upon them in the forceful way recorded in earlier chapters. Teachers, therefore, were forced to engage with the imperatives of the inspection at the same time as they were distancing themselves from it, though in large part the engage-ment was strategical rather than committed to the managerialist discourse.

Staging Performances

Goffman (1969) has written of how it is in the individual's interest

> to control the conduct of others, especially their responsive treatment of him [sic]. . . . This control is achieved largely by influencing the definition of the situation which the others come to formulate, and he can influence this definition by expressing himself in such a way as to give them the kind of impression that will lead them to act voluntarily in accordance with his own plan. (Ibid., p. 15)

The teachers engaged in some of this dramaturgical kind of activity, stag-ing performances to create a particular impression. Angelina (Lowstate) was convinced that 'we need to show off throughout Ofsted'. Laura (Lowstate) shows how during a pre-Ofsted visit by local inspectors, she switched from 'normal' to 'strategical' mode:

I knew he was coming in at quarter to 3 and I kept one eye on the clock and I was thinking, 'I'm not going to watch the door; I'm not going to watch the door', and I actually got engrossed in what I was doing and I wasn't aware of them coming in but once I knew they were in, I was conscious that I was performing for them — I wasn't teaching as I would have normally taught.

Frank (Cottingly) performed more spontaneously:

I played with fire in there. I'm my own worst enemy really. In assembly I asked if anybody ever had a good excuse for not doing anything — and talked about it. There was a little voice in my head saying 'but you don't know what they're going to come out with'. Playing it safe isn't really my nature. Just a bit of showing off when I really think of it.

Others performed to ensure survival: 'I resolved to pretend they weren't there.' Roger (Mixstead) was convinced that 'the inspectors wouldn't see normal life here. They won't know normality'. Glen (Flately) argued that his performance would 'depend on the inspectors' focus, and although I've done something the week before I will repeat it during inspection week to ensure that the children don't look as though they don't know what they're doing'. Leila (Flately) really enjoyed her self performing:

I was determined that they were going to see me in a lesson situation, that sort of situation that I do shine in, that would make me happy to do, because I get a big kick out of poetry and frankly I forgot about her sitting there, and the kids did as well. It was better than some that I'd done.

Shula (Flately) thought,

we had to blind them with science to be honest with you. I think we had so much and looked so prepared, so organized in relation to perhaps some other schools that I think they were just overwhelmed really in terms of what we had to show. We knew what the questions would be and we fitted our answers to them.

Rebecca, in the same school, also felt, 'We came out better than we thought we would but it was a show.' When Leila, again at the same school, was being monitored by her PE coordinator she

did everything I normally do but I did even more, I emphasized every-thing. That's what I'm trying to say. So in the classroom when Ofsted come we are going to be emphasizing everything. If I want it quiet we are going to try to be getting it even quieter. So Ofsted can go away with the impression that they are quiet, even though they probably are already. My local inspector has encouraged me to do that, so now I'm thinking when Ofsted come I'll be going around constantly doing this.

Teachers prepared their children. 'The children were keyed up. I deliberately told them I wanted them to be on their toes.' Angelina realized they had to prime the children to shine by saying, 'Oh look at this, look what I can do.' Amy (Lowstate) took control of the situation by 'giving Ofsted all the information they are likely to need. It's a show and I'm making it easy for them.' Reen (Mixstead) who normally revised for the SATs during the inspection term, with the 'tacit approval of the governors' (see Chapter 3), put that to one side to prepare an 'Ofsted performance':

> So, if you say 'Will it change my practice?' It will while they are here and it will put me six weeks behind with the training for this test; that is how I see it. I wouldn't say it's difficult because after you have been teaching 30 years as I have, you can swing into any action. I just feel it is like unwelcome in-laws turning up; that is how I feel about them, and I could do without them getting in my way and stopping me getting on with what I need to do which is constant revision.

Teachers also 'covered angles' by trying to ensure they couldn't get caught out. Rebecca (Flately) argued,

> What happens if they see a timetable for three weeks ago and a book with some maths in it with a different date on it or no maths dated for that week? Are they going to check up? I could say I didn't stick to the timetable. Is that rational to worry about this? Perhaps I ought to go and look back through my books matching the entries up with timetable. It's like a fairy story come true.

They also 'mugged up', by reading all the school's policies. Susanna (Flately) wanted to be prepared for the inspectors' questions,

> What makes me frightened is that maybe they will ask some questions to which I don't know the answers. Last year they asked me about reading policy and I couldn't give them any answer. I was just quiet. I want to know about reading policy this year; how we are following them. I know how we are following but I want to get the ideas from other classes.

In Susanna's school the teachers were provided with a list of possible questions and they held a workshop to practise the interview sessions. 'Talking up' was encouraged, but many teachers found this both unnatural and difficult. They wanted to show the best side of their work and the school, but this process could mean that they didn't address what they saw as weaknesses in their particular areas of responsibility. They also wanted to be seen as honest, open and reflective people. Many of them found the actual interview process difficult. They spoke of their inarticulateness and talked graphically about 'hating interviews' (Carol – Trafflon). The subject interviews in Flately were in teams, and overall this helped the teachers, though some felt that their influence on their subject development might not be noticed because of their shyness. One team in the school presented so much material to the inspectors that according to Leila 'they were flabbergasted and went away saying they had seen nothing like it before'. The team were very excited by their performance. 'It was brilliant; we really showed them.' Grace, her deputy head, went further and had a Senior Management Team meeting about achievement and monitoring and tried to anticipate their question. 'We practised ensuring that we presented a consensus for any interviews we had. It was very helpful. I want them to say that the Senior Management Team has a shared clear view. I don't want to be the one who balls it up.' Others imported lists of possible questions from other schools' INSET files. Two schools employed consultants to help teachers practice for their coordinators' interviews. This is in line with surveys that show that 40 per cent of primary schools spent an average of £500 on preparation (Rafferty and Dean, 1996). Grace's experience was that 'he fired things at you and made you think "I don't do that or that" and I'd feel in a panic but it helps in the long term knowing everything.'

They were keen on looking cool and ruling out problems. Helen (Cottingly) said to the school management, 'I really need the new hamster now if he's coming. I don't want it a week before Ofsted when the children are still likely to be high on it being there.' Bronwyn, of the same school, said 'I never had such well prepared lessons in my life. It's rather pathetic really'. In an observed maths lesson she

> was stage managing it so the inspectors could see that we were using the different resources that we had. You have to be confident enough to do that. They didn't know that I was shaking in my boots. I have this tremendous ability to appear so confident; nobody knows that really I'd been sick three times that one morning. I have that ability to appear so cool.

They manipulated situations, 'I kept them going to see band practices to keep them out of the classroom', admitted Raymond, the head of Flatley. Sophie, at the same school, took less risks and kept the children busy: 'They won't have a minute to spare — no choosing.' There were more class lessons and less movement around the classroom. The head at Cottingly encouraged her teachers 'to start the week with a good lesson to build confidence and determine the inspectors' perceptions', and there was some considerable disappointment when these were not observed by an inspector. Frank, at the same school, did not do his more 'bread and butter' lessons like spellings and handwriting and produced 'showy English lessons that I would have done during the term but there would not have been so many of them together'. Topics were timed to develop their most interesting phases during inspection week such as the construction of evacuation suitcases and in one class the importation of incubating chicken's eggs was held back to coincide with inspection week (though the chicks failed to cooperate). Teachers also avoided what they considered to be their weaker subjects: 'No way' was Frank 'going to do geography or music'; nor was Shula (Flately) going to 'do any drama'. However, some, like Frederica (Cottingly) grew resistant to the idea of presentation and performance: 'I'm not going to change my way of working. If they can do better let them try.' Even so, support teachers and pupils observed some changes in these teachers' approaches: 'The class teacher was tense and there was less humour in the classroom'; 'She was less funny and kept going on about a broken thermometer whereas normally she would have said "don't worry"'. Amy, who was commended by the inspectors, recognized teaching as performing and felt confident but she still focused on it during a pre-Ofsted visit:

> I'm an ex-trainer so I'm a bit used to performing in front of adults which makes it easier. I was doing this thing with the children about how you can't always believe what you see and you've got to have proof, and I was getting them to act little things out that were a bit ambiguous and say what they thought was happening, and it was going brilliantly. I then began to think 'He isn't bloody coming, he's late', and was conscious that this was good and he wasn't watching it. So I did an extra one and he arrived just at the end of the last one, so I just put another one in, which was pure performance for him. It's not what was necessary for the children. I was conscious that I was being judged, assessed. It feeds into the bit of me that judges me rather too much.

They also passed on the pressure at times, albeit reluctantly. Shona (Flately) pushed her children 'to finish things ready for the week whereas last term I had spent building a team spirit in the class'. Lois, the head at Lowstate, pressurized parents, summoning them to a meeting a few weeks before the SATs just prior to the inspection and told them that their children were not achieving well enough in the SATs.

The irony of the situation was that many were not at their best during the inspection. This was less to do with the inspection week ('all I've got to do this week is teach'), but tiredness was a major consequence of the build up to it, 'That's the most boring lesson I've ever taught. I was so tired.' Their performance was also affected by having the inspectors in the room as Sophie (Flately) was 'still nervous, of them coming in. I know my voice will go a bit wobbly and if I'm talking on the carpet I'll think, "Oh dear, I just want to get this over and done with"'. Sherina (Flately), a very confident teacher, became somewhat tearful when she realized it was her class assembly during the inspection week (though it was highly praised and she was thrilled with the children's performances having spent some considerable time perfecting it). Freda (Cottingly), who was normally an enthusiastic, jolly, calm teacher, by her own reckoning, also with four years' experience, left her assembly preparation to the last week prior to the inspection. She had been busy with a great deal of extra curricula activity and was determined, like many teachers in her school, to try to continue the normal school routines, but when she did attend to the whole process of assembly planning and production it became the worst moment of her teaching career. 'It is hell', she uttered. She became ill; worked every night till past 7 o'clock in school and ended up very miserable on the Sunday night prior to the inspection. 'I broke down in tears to my dad on the phone at 11 o'clock the night before the inspection. He was a deputy head and he thought it was terrible.'

Assertiveness

Teachers defended themselves to inspectors in case they got the wrong idea. Esther (Lowstate), had a pupil saying, 'Oh, I don't know what I'm supposed to do'. She was

> afraid that she (the inspector) was thinking, 'This woman (the teacher) is not getting him work to do'. I thought, 'I'm not having her thinking the wrong thing', and I said to the pupil 'Look, what are you doing? I told you to get your book out and bring it to me so that I could put your work in it', and he went to get his book and I said to her, 'This child is statemented; he's supposed to have 10 helper hours a week which he doesn't get and he's very attention-seeking; that's why he's behaving like this'.

Laura at the same school 'talked herself up'

> about how fine I feel and how I enjoy the work, because other people need a bit of uplift, and I go in and talk to someone who's getting really wound up and try and say, 'your room's great', and it is, and she hasn't got anything to worry about.

Lional (Lowstate) described how his school culture was assertive, 'That's something that we have always said to ourselves anyway. You hear it said at staff meetings; you hear it said across the staff room, that we think we're okay. I would say that is the coping strategy at the moment — I think they're prepared to say that they feel that what they're doing is all right.' Carol (Trafflon) was determined 'to say that the individual counts here and that we actually look at individuals and we look at the progress that they make and I'm determined to get that in somehow and that we've reviewed our policies'.

Teachers asserted their superiority in practical teaching. Sophie (Flately) thought 'they may have all the gift of the gab and they might be able to tell us all the theory and tell us how it should be done but I'd like to see them actually do it. So in some ways I feel a bit superior to them because I feel that our job is more important than theirs'. Toni (Trafflon) intoned to herself on the first day of the inspection, 'I'm better than any of them on my worst day.' They had strong self belief. Kirsty (Mixstead) claimed that 'everyone has an inner self-esteem. I don't like to feel I'm not doing well'. Becky (Cottingly) said,

> Although you could make a complete hash of something you're good at, when there's somebody else there I don't feel inadequate. I believe I'm a good teacher, that my children do well. . . . Yes, it's part of school life now but it's not going to ruin three quarters of a year's work just for two weeks of panic or whatever. I think you've got to believe in yourself.

Sometimes, the feeling of superiority was not enough. Formal complaint was required on occasion. Elaine (Lowstate) for example,

> was so angry and I wanted to sort of hit out, and then as the week went on I sort of got to the stage where I thought, 'I don't care; it doesn't matter; I know that I'm good at my job and all that so it doesn't matter.' Then I thought, 'Blow me, I do!' and then I started to put this letter together on the computer and thought, 'I will let them know how I feel because it's important to me.'

At other times, teachers developed a 'bottom line', and were determined to resist any attempt to drop below that line. Veronica (Trafflon) argued that her 'safety barrier is that she can walk out and tell the inspector what to think'. She was not so restricted by the corporateness of the situation. Other bottom lines, like Aileen's (Lowstate) were to do with survival, 'I just don't want to fail. I don't care who gets commended. I just don't want to fail.' Letica's bottom line was even more drastic: ' "What's the worst they can do?" my sister said. "You could lose your job but we wouldn't let you become destitute" '. However, she was very relieved when she wasn't picked out for criticism.

Veronica's (Trafflon) general feelings of fear of being designated a failure due to her childhood experiences at the hands of her father, were overcome when cornered. She challenged an inspector who was later reprimanded for questioning her teaching methods. 'I don't do it intentionally because it slipped out, because normally I walk away. I don't even listen to it but I couldn't go anywhere, could I? I was in my classroom. Well, where could I walk to?'

There were noticeable attempts to break down the tense relationships through humanizing the situation. Gayle (Flately) was determined to get some control over the process and so she acknowledged each inspector as they came into the room and tried to establish a human connection. 'I felt better about them being there after I had done that.' She also had a bad start to the week, apart from suffering from flu, when her PE lesson did not start well. She talked of a sinking feeling' and then of a 'voice telling her what to do'. She stopped the lesson and talked to the children about having visitors in the hall. This she described as a necessary step if 'she were going to survive the week'.

Playing the Game

There was a certain amount of accepting the inevitable, but without enthusiasm. Evelyn (Mixstead) accepted the need for assessment: 'It's part of life. It's an expected way of life'. Angelina (Lowstate) accepted that some would receive grades and others would not: 'We're not all excellent, or we're not all bright or what? We're the same as the vast majority of the world; we're average, but we're good.' She thinks the new inspection system 'divisive and I don't like it, but I'm not in a position to alter it. And I'm not going to waste my energy. I get on with doing what I'm good at, which is teaching children and it's them that count'. She is ambivalent: 'I'm not saying it's right and I'm not saying it's wrong; I'm saying it's a fact of life.' Gloria (Flately), who did get nervous and distressed at one point in spite of her confidence in her own teaching, didn't resent it. 'I don't resent it. It's just something you had to go through'. Dan (Morghouse) did not want to engage in the rights and wrongs of the event, 'I don't know if this is the way to do it but that's the system.' Esther (Lowstate) just 'does it . . . and if you have to make it up, you make it up'.

'Playing the game' was a central part of the process. Georgina (Flately) argued that they needed to be aware of Ofsted's demands, then 'you try to give them what they want to see . . . once it's over we'll all revert to being normal again and talking about the things that are important'. Angelina (Lowstate) commenting on those who were commended thought that

> those people rose to the occasion or played the game better. It's a team sport, facing Ofsted. They (the highly graded) scored a few goals, that's all. It doesn't mean to say that the rest of the team aren't any good, does it? You still need a goalkeeper at the other end to stop the goals going in. Probably me!

Raymond, the head at Flately, found himself caught up in a game he didn't really want to be in but with which he had to engage. He had virtually no choice but to agree to a newspaper report of his good inspection report put out by the local authority:

> I knew that by going public like that I was entering into the whole competition game, as it were, but I felt that because we were in the game then the staff and the school and the kids and the parents ought to get the recognition if it was going. I'm not interested in that competition culture at all, but we're in it.

There is a price to be paid, therefore, for strategic engagement. In spite of being assertive in an inspection encounter as shown above, Veronica (Trafflon) resented 'what I've done. I've never compromised before and I feel ashamed. It's like licking their boots'. For Diane (Morghouse) it was a sad experience in that she lost respect for herself:

> My first reaction was 'I'm not going to play the game', but I am and I know they know I am. I don't respect myself for it; my own self respect goes down. Why aren't I making a stand? Why aren't I saying, 'I know I can teach; say what you want to say', and so I lose my own self-respect. I know who I am; I know why I teach, and I don't like it; I don't like them doing this, and that's sad, isn't it?

Tracy (Lowstate) believed that

> you've got to sell yourself because we didn't show ourselves. So we should show them we've always done this and there it is for you to see; bring it all out; it's been hidden, like we've put it in a folder; we've put it away somewhere. Because Ofsted is coming, now you've got to keep everything. . . . They're making you sell yourself by building it up into something fantastic, something great, unknown thing — some fear — some big thing is happening and you've got to show how wonderful you are, how wonderful this school is and everything, when it's always wonderful.

Georgina (Flately) argued that they are spending less time on children's progress. 'Last year we were asking, "why is this child here and that child there and what can we do to move them forward"'. Now I'll be saying 'well if they want to see science I will teach science', I'll teach the plan. Once that's over we'll revert to being normal again.

Carol (Trafflon) had 'got resigned in some ways. There's just no escape is there really? They've got a remit; you've got to fit in with it or you are absolutely stuffed, because if they are not happy the HMIs will be in. There is no way you can say you don't agree with this; you've got to do it'. Esther (Lowstate) agreed: 'I've decided I've just got to get through it, like most unpleasant things in life; you've just got to get through it, just pretend it's not happening though I'm not sure I know how to do that. At least, once done, it's done.' Lois, the head at Lowstate, was 'a great believer that it's behind us, so I've worked very much to be with everybody to accentuate positives from now on and look forward. We won't discuss the report in the staff meeting, only in the senior management team'.

The inspection was described as a 'painful experience to survive', or 'like preparing for an exam'. It was a matter of 'grinding on' to the end of the event, immersing themselves in the minutest detail of preparation. 'We've just got to get on with it.' Others were concerned with self preservation. Letica (Lowstate) described her relief at realizing she was not the focus of some criticism by the local inspector in a staff meeting: 'Thank God it's not me, you think.' There is a sense of relief that you have survived. 'I feel as if I can do things now that I couldn't before; I can focus on other areas of my life.'

Some felt inoculated: 'If there is a next time, I think I will be better equipped to cope with it myself.' However, memories of the inspections a year or more later in the same schools were just as traumatic (see Chapter 3). Sometimes teachers invested in the inspection as an inoculation against family circumstances as Enid (Mixstead) indicated after the painful death of her mother, 'so while I am busy it doesn't worry me too much, probably in the holiday I will notice it more; we are kept busy'.

Appropriation

Some teachers not only went along with, resisted or confronted the discourse but also 'appropriated' parts of it. 'To appropriate is to take over, to use as one's own. . . . to further (one's) own ends, even though in some particulars its values seem diametrically opposed' (Woods, 1995, p. 64). The Ofsted process was a new experience for primary schools, one in which teachers could see that there might be some advantages for them, particularly where they were able to take up the language and practice of what they could see was an influential discourse. This could in some cases assist promotion but it could also be beneficial to any identity that was bound closely to the corporate culture of the institution (Casey, 1995). Some teachers enjoyed the new planning schedules and some found the timetables to their liking.

The inspection process was also used by management but also by some post holders to develop their own ideas. One head used the good report for further recruitment of pupils. Other reasons for investing in engagement were for career and professional development. Thus, Gayle (Flately) took the opportunity to improve her pedagogic skills by visiting other classes prior to the inspection. Shereena, at the same school, took the opportunity to enhance the profile of music in the school and her own expertise.

Some teachers ensured that their presentational skills were honed, as Larry (Lowstate) indicates:

> There is a skill in being pro-active toward inspectors by looking at the positives with them. I think to do your preparation as a coordinator for a meeting is time well spent. The whole pressure on teachers is about being able to be articulate and to speak well about what you're doing. I do think we need to think about that. We're in a new climate.

Larry argued that

> It is up to you as to whether you want to jump through those hoops. . . .
> I had the chance to talk to someone who obviously has visited a lot of

schools and they gave a couple of suggestions or said that's fine. Looking at me as an individual, with the marks I got I thought I was doing a good job and what I was doing was good and it was nice to have that confirmed. It's not often you get the opportunity to get someone to come in and say 'Yes you are doing a good job.'

Teachers were instrumental in their actions, for example bringing the classroom fish tank into their curriculum that week. They overcame some of the challenges that were presented and felt better for it. Lois (Lowstate) developed her management role in line with other heads (Sandbrook, 1996; Ouston et al., 1996; Wilcox and Gray, 1996). 'The handbook is a good model; it has made me think about my management role. My role is to support staff and I can see the advantages of doing this within the audit model of monitoring classroom activity.' They focused on controlling small details as Rebecca (Flately) argued, 'We can't control the big things so we try to control the small things. We can't just say "we can't do anything", we need to do something.' Angelina (Lowstate)

would rather have not have done it because it hasn't told us anything that we don't know. But I feel more positive now after doing it. It gives us evidence to say, 'Well, we've got to do something about Key Stage 1' and this is what we're going to do about it. We need another teacher and we're going to target our primary helpers down there. We could quietly have just left things.

Carol (Trafflon) had had some good SATs results the following year and

every child who took the writing and reading test this year went through our school from the very beginning and I find that kind of thing very comforting because Ofsted used results based on a lot of children who had moved into the area and came midway through their schooling. So that does boost my confidence because we can say that this confirms what we knew already.

Gloria (Flately) used the good report to confirm her own skills: 'It reminded you of when you first started teaching as well, when you had to have everything set up just so because you were so lacking in confidence, you needed the re-assurance that your organization and your planning and everything was absolutely right'. Larry had sharpened his practice through being more explicit about his aims and objectives:

I say at the beginning of a lesson 'what I want you to get out of this by the end of it'. I never used to do that. I used to assume that they would empathize with me and understand these things as if by magic. I just think that I am giving them clearer goals than I probably ever have done in my teaching career so far. . . . That timetable wouldn't have been there prior Ofsted; it's there and it's real, it's not Mickey Mouse. I worked it; I'm happier; the kids are happier and I genuinely think it works.

There was some personal adjustment (Becker, 1964), whereby the individual actually changes, forced rather than voluntary. The most dramatic case was that of Cloe. She was the only year 6 teacher at Trafflon and after criticism of their SATs results she resolved to go down the path of 'improvement of results'. She changed her curriculum, and achieved her aim by getting the second best results the following year in her LEA. She justified this by saying that she was 'now just doing a job', and had withdrawn her total involvement to preserve her 'sanity'. 'The results were better because I acted like a function machine. It wasn't much fun. I just went at it like a steam train. I went through the whole of the science curriculum as we were taught it at school. So they learnt examination skills. They learnt the facts, questions that might come up and they learnt skills. . . . Judged by the Ofsted criteria if I was graded I'd be a star pupil.' She has coped by making this adjustment but it is not to her liking:

> All of us are having to change our practice in the classroom and move further and further away from the school we are in and more and more towards what is happening in secondary schools. Unless you actually do it that way you can't get through the curriculum. I don't enjoy it.

Teachers re-asserted themselves, after the event, like Gayle (Flately) who reverted to her favoured style: 'I didn't make my kids relentlessly carry on with an ongoing task, we work for two and a half hours in the morning and two and a half hours in the afternoon because I think it's quite unhealthy for kids of this age to do so. I was going back to my old ways. There was a lot of hype that week and the following week was like a dream.' They re-structured themselves, as did George at the same school:

> I did consider at some time whether it was worth carrying on but then I've trained all my life for this. This is what I want to do, so it's either a case of taking charge of the situation or just getting out of it. So I suppose I'm looking now to try and find ways of dealing with it. I think it did take a lot out of me. I don't think it necessarily created enjoyment for me but now I'm looking to find ways of actually enjoying it more again.

Shula did this through a new approach to a topic. 'I'm reconstructing now. . . . I was in turmoil because I wasn't expressing myself in any way that I felt was creative because my definitions had gone. . . . It wasn't my choice, it was outside influences. The Ofsted really shook me but it might well have been a good thing, in the sense that it made me start to kick back and say, "No way, no way, I'm not sitting back and taking this".'

Conclusion

In these ways, teachers are not just coping in the limited sense of reacting to the inspection within the constraints of the discourse, but are re-creating the event in their own terms and actively reconstructing the discourse itself. Their methods are various, and some seem in opposition to others. Menter et al. (1997) suggest that some teachers may be 'living out the consequences of change in terms of fractured and fragmented identities' (p. 115). Some may see them in consequence as passive victims of a dominant structural process. The evidence presented in this chapter suggests a more active involvement in the reconstruction of their identities. Teachers have multi-faceted, rather than fragmented, selves, and they demonstrate considerable skill at developing and employing strategies to match particular situations. This apparent strategical switching is best explained, we argue, through the concept of 'positioning'. Davies argues that there is something specifically 'positional' about conversation within and between discourses:

> The newly emerging view is that in learning to talk, and thus to use the discursive practices that are available within the social world, each person gains access to what it means to be a person within each of the discourses available to them and in practising them becomes the kind of speaker who is implicated in and made sense of through such practices. (Davies, 1990, p. 342)

In other words, what goes on in conversations is a matter of continual positioning either by the dominant participant or the other, both positioning themselves according to the nature of the engagement and the use of appropriation of the discourse.

> In addition, each person beings to any episode of collaborative constitution of the world in this or that way, their accumulated personal history — their sense of themselves not only as they were positioned in the present moment but also of themselves as persons who can or cannot be positioned in that way, i.e. as one who is located in certain ways within the social and moral order, who is known to act and feel in certain ways, whose life is explicable within known story lines. (Davies, 1990, p. 342)

Teachers position themselves among a number of different discourses such as 'child centredness', 'realities', or managerialism according to their own biographies. To our teachers, inspectors' actions seem positioned within one discourse, that of managerialism (though see Chapter 1). Applying the argument to women, Davies (1992, p. 56) claims

> Once they. . . . see how they are positioned within the various discourses through which they are constituted, they can begin to refuse

some of those positionings and along with them some of the particular discourse in which those positionings are embedded. The issue ceases to be the vulnerability of the essential female self attempting to do that which history says she cannot do. It becomes instead the analysis of discursive practices and the finding of ways to collectively resist the constitution of women inside the male/female dualism.

Kenway et al. (1994, p. 102) also argue that

Girls' identities are shifting and fragmented, multiple and contradictory, displaced and positioned as they are across the various discourses which historically and currently constitute their lives in and out of school. . . . This post-structuralist view of identity encourages gender reformers to recognize all girls (boys, teachers) as complex human beings and as active readers of their cultures . . . and it allows us all to better appreciate and understand the many questions and dilemmas which girls (boys, teachers) face at school.

It is not, therefore, a matter of coming to objective conclusions about successful or failing teachers, or what constitutes a 'proper' or 'good' teacher, but analysing the discourses, reconstituting one's own, 'reading the story lines' and re-empowering the self, sometimes 'against the grain'.

We need not only to see the problems in rational, didactic terms (though we need that too) but to see freshly the images and metaphors and story lines we have grown up with and to learn to read them against the grain. (Davies, 1992, p. 74)

In order to do this, we must be able to identify the 'grain'. It is what we would expect of professionals. In devising the strategies described here, teachers are reasserting their professional selves, so threatened in the emotional upheavals described in Chapter 4. But they do it in various ways, positioning themselves among different discourses according to their own interests and personal resources. For example, Angelina (Lowstate) felt teaching was a mission, accepted realities, played the game and acted instrumentally. Carol (Trafflon) felt the process unfair; her family relations were damaged, but, still lacking confidence, she 'mugged up', and asserted herself. Cloe (Trafflon) knew it was an impossible job, that teaching was complex, but she felt alone and in the end she capitulated and distanced herself from her past values unlike Larry (Lowstate) who appropriated the process for his own enhancement.

Ofsted's purpose is 'to improve standards of achievement and quality of education through regular independent inspection, public reporting and informed advice' (Ofsted, 1995). Questions that might be asked are: How far are the consequences described in this chapter promoting that aim? What are the consequences for children's education of this diversion of teacher creativity to strategical activity?

Notes from the Field (6)
Friday — Celebration and Review

As I arrive in the school at 9.45 a.m. I am informed by support staff that there are some tension points and there have been some tears from one quarter. 'That's why it's wrong. They work their hardest and get criticized.' There's a rough large notice on the staffroom table 'It's official: We are a good school' and this is supplemented by an A4 computer printed message

Lowstate Ofsted
Good School

1996
Primary School

Well Done Everyone

which looks similar to a medal and a copy is spotted adorning the wall in the school office. A visitor remarks 'You did well then. Is this the highest category — the gold star?' At breaktime the headteacher gives a verbal report back to the staff and I volunteer for break duty, for to stay would be a surveillance too far. However, I am informed that there is 'fall out' already though this is not elaborated upon. One of the teachers who found the experience positive says jokingly to me 'I've got a taste for this. I fancy getting another fix and going somewhere that's having an Ofsted.'

The headteacher is concerned about the grading of teachers in terms of the diminution of her power but also because she feels that some of the inspectors don't like it either. 'Many of the inspectors have had no choice but to become Ofsted inspectors.' However, much of this relaxation of relations may be based on relief at receiving a good report.

One tension point involves the non recognition by the inspectors of a non-teacher who plays a major role in one department. The persons concerned are very annoyed and they attempt to get things changed and later they take the matter to a professional association. The incident causes some considerable tension this morning between one worker and the head which the latter is unable to resolve immediately. The other tension concerns the 'excellent' grading commendations which some teachers feel is divisive, and the inspectors' methods are questioned in some detail for there are different perspectives on the validity of the awards. In the light of these awards some teachers are heard to mutter 'What does that say about me then?' Staff wish to know whether the head has access to individual teacher grades.

At lunchtime there is much discussion about the negative aspects of inspection and the unfairness of the critical comments made about the two teachers, and in other places in the school there is concern about the effects of the 'excellent' gradings. One of the criticised teachers, Tracy, puts a card on the staffroom table: 'Thank you everyone for your support through my "downs". This is becoming rather a habit don't you think? You're a sport. Love Tracy.' It's a sad end to her week which began with so much optimism and enthusiasm from her. At the other end of the scale the teacher who enjoyed the event comments: 'If one is not anxious does that mean the process is less intensified or there is less involvement? No, it means better outcomes and a saner response to the whole process.'

At 4 p.m. most of the staff, including the support staff, adjourn to a local pub where a room has been set aside for a celebration with a large buffet and large rounds of drinks are bought by the management. The party goes on till after 8 p.m. and there they relax, make presentations to the head and deputy, tell tales of the event and evaluate the process. I get a sound bite evaluation of the inspection from each one of them. Nine were critical, three recognised some good in amongst the disadvantages and one found it enjoyable:

> Pressurised, pressurised. I didn't like it at the end — I was looking forward to it but in the end it was demoralising, demoralising. They didn't try to find out the reason why some children behaved the way they did. I just wonder what they do with the information they've got. It ought to be something positive. But anyway, I'm not going to let it bother me or anything because I know the way I work is OK, so does everybody else. (Tracy)

> I don't want to say anything, thank you. You see, this Ofsted situation has simply emphasized and re-emphasized the divide in the school. What upset me was to see one of the best people in the school hurt. (Ava)

> A waste of time, energy and I would also say I think it was worthless and valueless. (Letica)

It seems like they made pretty early judgments, and then they go back to the ones they think they want to commend or criticize. (Edith)

I think it's horrendous and I've only been in for one day of it. I just don't think I'd like to go through that again for a very long time! I don't see the point in it — they didn't tell us anything we didn't already know and I think people have been absolutely exhausted by it. (Leila)

I think in any kind of constructive sense it was a non-event. I don't see what we got out of it. It hasn't changed my view of it at all and I just think, 'Why are we doing it?' It confirms my feelings that it's got a political agenda. It's nothing to do with making education better for children or giving teachers guidance about being better, it's a stick. (Amy)

Exhausting, very negative, I don't ever want to go through all that again — it was dreadful, absolutely dreadful. (Esther)

It hasn't helped. A waste of time, didn't tell me anything I didn't already know, I think it's been divisive, I think it's been demoralising, I think it's not left us any happier than we were before. (Aileen)

They could have given that money to the school for resources instead of having all six walk around. They were only really here for criticism, weren't they? I know two have got excellent marks, but it doesn't help the youngsters and they all work hard. (Support Worker)

I don't know why we've done it. I suppose in some ways it's confirmed our professional judgment so perhaps that in itself is good. I think it has highlighted some weaknesses and we've got to be a little bit more proactive for the Key Stage I. However, mainly a waste of time. I don't feel particularly anything about it at the moment. I feel jet-lagged I think. Last night was the only night I didn't sleep. I felt as though my body was catching up with my mind, it's so peculiar, it's weird — it's like when you've been on an aeroplane and you're in a different time zone. I don't feel happy or ecstatic about it. I don't know that I feel anything particularly at the moment, a bit numb I suppose. (Angelina)

I'm relieved it's all over. I don't know that I've learnt anything very much that I didn't know before, nice to be re-assured that what we're doing is okay I suppose but then I was 99 per cent sure of that anyway. It could have been nastier, the people were very obliging, very polite, very helpful, tried to be unintrusive — bit of a shame about the stress that some people have been put through. I felt a certain amount of stress myself, I guess we all have, but some people have felt it more than others. One or two people have got rather down feelings as a result of it all which I think is a bit unfair and a bit unnecessary. (Lional)

I feel it was a positive exercise and it's done me a lot of good. It's made me feel better about myself. The build-up was hell but they were quite nice people actually. (Lola)

It was a doddle, no problem — I'd do it again tomorrow. Very positive experience. (Laura)

The following week is half term and two of the teachers are off to Morocco the following day. One is off walking, another goes off to a cottage for the week-end and the head goes down to her country home. One of the commended teachers is to spend the first few days working on a presentation to be given at the end of the week and the others mostly plan to stay close to home. The event is over, the school is calm and quiet again, until next time.

References

Acker, S. (1990) 'Teachers culture in an English primary school: Continuity and change', *British Journal of Sociology of Education*, **11**, 3, pp. 257–74.

Acker, S. (1994) *Gendered Education*, Buckingham: Open University Press.

Alexander, R. (1992) *Policy and Practice in Primary Education*, London: Routledge.

Alexander, R. (1995) *Versions of Primary Education*, London: Routledge.

Apple, M.W. (1986) *Teachers and Texts: A Political Economy of Class and Gender Relations in Education*, New York: Routledge and Kegan Paul.

Apple, M.W. and Jungck, S. (1992) 'You don't have to be a teacher to teach this unit: Teaching, technology and control in the curriculum', in Hargreaves, A. and Fullan, M. (eds) *Understanding Teacher Development*, London: Cassell, pp. 20–42.

Armon-Jones, C. (1986) 'The social functions of emotions', in Harré, R. (ed.) *The Social Construction of Emotions*, Oxford: Basil Blackwell, pp. 57–82.

Aspland, R. and Brown, G. (1993) 'Keeping teaching professional', in Bridges, D. and Kerry, T. (eds) *Developing Teachers Professionally*, London: Routledge, pp. 6–22.

Ball, S.J. (1990a) *Politics and Policy Making in Education: Explorations in Policy Sociology*, London: Routledge.

Ball, S.J. (1990b) (ed.) *Foucault and Education: Disciplines and Knowledge*, London: Routledge.

Ball, S.J. (1994) *Education Reform: A Critical and Post-structural Approach*, Buckingham: Open University Press.

Ball, S.J. and Bowe, R. (1992) 'Subject departments and the implementation of National Curriculum policy: An overview of the issues', *Journal of Curriculum Studies*, **24**, 2, pp. 97–115.

Barnard, N. (1997) 'The eunuchs' taskmaster', *Times Educational Supplement*, 1 August, London, p. 5.

B.B.C. (1995) 'The Inspection' *Modern Times*, 15 November.

Becker, H.S. (1964) 'Personal change in adult life', *Sociometry*, **27**, 1, pp. 40–53, also in Cosin, B., Dale, R., Esland, I.R., MacKinnon, G.M and Swift, D.F. (eds) (1977) *School and Society* (2nd ed.) London: Routledge and Kegan Paul.

Berger, P.L., Berger, B. and Kellner, H. (1973) *The Homeless Mind*, Harmondsworth: Penguin.

Bell. S. (1995) 'Oftos cartoons', *The Guardian*, November, London, p. 13.

Bonnett, M. (1994) *Children's Thinking: Promoting Understanding in the Primary School*, London: Cassell.

Bradney, P. (1957) 'The joking relationship in industry', *Human Relations*, **10**.

Braverman, H. (1974) Labour and Monopoly Capital. New York. Monthly Review Press.

References

Brimblecombe, N., Ormiston, M. and Shaw, M. (1995) 'Teachers' perceptions of school inspection: A stressful experience', *Cambridge Journal of Education*, **25**, 1, pp. 53–61.

Campbell, R.J. and Neill, S.R. St J. (1994a) *Primary Teachers at Work*, London: Routledge.

Campbell, R.J. and Neill, S.R. St J. (1994b) *Curriculum Reform at Key Stage 1: Teacher Commitment and Policy Failure*, Harlow: Longman Group UK.

Casey, C. (1995) *Work, Self and Society*, London: Routledge.

Casey, K. and Apple, M.W. (1989) 'Gender and the conditions of teachers' work: The development of understanding in America', in Acker, S. (ed.) *Teachers, Gender and Careers*, Lewes: Falmer Press.

Cooper, P. and McIntyre, D. (1996) *Effective Teaching and Learning: Teachers' and Students' Perspectives*, Buckingham: Open University Press.

Coser, R.L. (1958) 'Authority and decision making in a hospital: A comparative analysis', *American Sociological Review*, **23**, pp. 56–63.

Centre for the Study of Secondary Schools (1994) *Inspection: Improving Schools Together*, Queens Building, University of Leicester, Northampton.

Davies, A.F. (1989) *The Human Element: Three Essays in Political Psychology*, Harmondsworth: Penguin.

Davies, B. (1990) 'Agency as a form of discursive practice. A classroom scene observed', *British Journal of Sociology of Education*, **11**, 3, pp. 341–61.

Davies, B. (1992) 'Women's subjectivity and feminist stories', in Ellis, C. and Flaherty, M.G. (eds) *Investigating Subjectivity: Research on Lived Experience*, London: Sage, pp. 53–76.

Dean, J. (1995) 'What teachers and headteachers think about inspection', *Cambridge Journal of Education*, **25**, 1, pp. 45–52.

Demaine, J. (1988) 'Teachers' work, curriculum and the New Right', *British Journal of Sociology of Education*, **9**, 3, pp. 274–64.

Densmore, K. (1987) 'Professionalism, proletarianisation and teachers' work', in Popkewitz, T. (ed.) *Critical Studies in Teacher Education*, Lewes: Falmer Press, pp. 130–60.

Elliot, J. (1991) *Action Research for Educational Change*, Milton Keynes: Open University Press.

Emerson, J. (1969) 'Negotiating the serious import of humour', *Sociometry*, **32**, pp. 169–81.

Evans, L., Packwood, A., Neill, S.R. St J. and Campbell, R.J. (1994) *The Meaning of Infant Teachers' Work*, London: Routledge.

Fitz, J., Halpin, D. and Power, S. (1994) 'Implementation research and education policy: Practice and prospects', *British Journal of Educational Studies*, **42**, 1, pp. 53–69.

Fitz-Gibbon, C.T. (1995) 'Mental cruelty and inadequate methodology?', *Education Today and Tomorrow*, **47**, 2, pp. 6–7.

Fitz-Gibbon, C.T. (1996) *Monitoring Education: Indicators, Quality and Effectiveness*, London: Cassell.

Fitz-Gibbon, C.T. and Stephenson, N.J. (1996) *Evaluating Ofsted's Methodology* (draft report) University of Durham.

Foucault, M. (1977) *Discipline and Punish: The Birth of the Prison*, New York: Pantheon Books.

Foucault, M. (1979) *Discipline and Punish*, Harmondsworth: Penguin.

Foucault, M. (1980) *Power/Knowledge: Selected Interviews and Other Writings*, in Gordon, C. (ed.) New York: Pantheon.

FOUCAULT, M. (1988) 'The political technology of individuals', in MARTIN, L.H., GUTMAN, H. and HUTTON, P.H. (eds) *Technologies of the Self: A Seminar with Michel Foucault*, Amherst: The University of Massachusetts Press.

GARDINER, J. (1997) 'Woodhead wants to see more sacked', *Times Educational Supplement, 18 July, p. 5*, London, The Times Supplements.

GIDDENS, A. (1985) *The Nation State and Violence*, Cambridge: Polity.

GILROY, P. and WILCOX, B. (1997) 'OFSTED, criteria and the nature of social understanding: A Wittgensteinian critique of the practice of educational judgement', *British Journal of Educational Studies*, **45**, 1, pp. 22–38.

GIPPS, C., BROWN, M., MCCALLUM, B. and MCALLISTER, S. (1995) *Intuition or Evidence?: Teachers and National Assessment of Seven-Year-Olds*, Buckingham: Open University Press.

GOFFMAN, E. (1961) *Encounters*, New York: Bobbs-Merrill.

GOFFMAN, E. (1968) *Asylums*, Harmondsworth: Penguin.

GOFFMAN, E. (1969) *The Presentation of Self in Everyday Life*, Harmondsworth: Penguin.

GRACE, G. (1985) 'Judging teachers: The social and political contexts of teacher evaluation', *British Journal of Sociology of Education*, **6**, 1, pp. 3–16.

HABERMAS, J. (1972) *Towards A Rational Society*, London: Heineman.

HACKETT, G. (1995) 'Woodhead castigates progressives', *The Guardian*, 27 January, p. 3.

HAIGH, G. (1996) 'Teachers and acute anxiety over preparation for inspection', *Times Educational Supplement*, 19 April, London, p. 3.

HAMMERSLEY, M. (1992) *What's Wrong with Ethnography? Methodological Explorations*, London: Routledge.

HAMMERSLEY, M. (1997) 'Educational research and teaching: A response to David Hargreaves', (Draft): Open University.

HARGREAVES, A. (1994) *Changing Teachers, Changing Times: Teachers' Work and Culture in the Post-modern age*, London: Cassell.

HARGREAVES, D.H. (1980) 'A sociological critique of individualism', *British Journal of Educational Studies*, **28**, 3, pp. 187–98.

HARGREAVES, D.H. (1983) 'The teaching of art and the art of teaching: Towards an alternative view of aesthetic learning', in HAMMERSLEY, M. and HARGREAVES, A. (eds) *Curriculum Practice: Some Sociological Case Studies*, Lewes: Falmer Press, pp. 127–47.

HARGREAVES, D.H. (1994) 'The new professionalism: The synthesis of professional and institutional development', *Teaching and Teacher Education*, **10**, 4, pp. 423–38.

HARRÉ, R. (1986) (ed.) *The Social Construction of Emotions*, Oxford: Basil Blackwell.

HARTLEY, D. (1994) 'Mixed messages in education policy: Sign of the times?' *British Journal of Educational Studies*, **42**, 3, pp. 230–44.

HATCHER, R. (1994) 'Market relationships and the management of teachers', *British Journal of Sociology of Education*, **15**, 1, pp. 41–62.

HENKEL, M. (1991) *Government, Evaluation and Change*, London: Jessica Kingsley.

JONES, K. (1989) *Right Turn: The Conservative Revolution in Education*, London: Hutchinson Radius.

KEDDIE, N. (1971) 'Classroom knowledge', in YOUNG, M. (ed.) *Knowledge and Control: New Directions in the Sociology of Education*, West Drayton: Collier Macmillan.

KENWAY, J.S., WILLIS, J., BLACKMORE, J. and RENNIE, L. (1994) 'Making hope practical' rather than 'despair convincing': Feminist post-structuralism, gender reform and educational change', *British Journal of Sociology of Education*, **15**, 2, pp. 187–210.

KICKERT, W. (1991) 'Steering at a distance: A new paradigm of public governance in Dutch higher education', paper for the European Consortium for Political Research, University of Essex, March.

LAW, J. (1994) *Organizing Modernity*, Oxford and Cambridge, Mass.: Blackwell.

LEE, J. and FITZ, J. (1997) 'HMI and Ofsted: Evolution or revolution in school inspection', *British Journal of Educational Studies*, **45**, 1, pp. 39–52.

MAGUIRE, M. and BALL, S.J. (1994) 'Researching politics and the politics of research: Recent qualitative studies in the UK', *International Journal of Qualitative Studies in Education*, **7**, 3, pp. 269–85.

MAW, J. (1995) 'The handbook for the inspection of schools: A critique', *Cambridge Journal of Education*, **25**, 1, pp. 75–88.

McLAREN, P. (1986) *Schooling As a Ritual Performance*, London: Routledge and Kegan Paul.

MEALYEA, R. (1989) 'Humour as a coping strategy', *British Journal of Sociology of Education*, **10**, 3, pp. 311–33.

MENTER, I., MUSCHAMP, Y., NICHOLLS, P., OZGA, J. and POLLARD, A. (1997) *Work and Identity in the Primary School*, Buckingham: Open University Press.

MILLER, J. (1996) *School for Women*, London: Virago.

MILLS, C.W. (1959) *The Sociological Imagination*, New York: Oxford University Press.

MONTGOMERY, J. (1996) ' "Shoddy" lessons come under fire', *Times Educational Supplement*, 5 July, London, p. 16.

MUSGROVE, F.M. (1977) *Margins of the Mind*, London: Methuen.

NEWMAN, J. and CLARKE, J. (1994) 'Going about our business?: The managerialization of public services', in CLARKE, J., COCHRANE, A. and McLAUGHLIN, E. (eds) *Managing Social Policy*, London: Sage.

NIAS, J. (1989) *Primary Teachers Talking*, London: Routledge.

NIAS, J. (1993) 'Changing times, changing identities: grieving for a lost self', in BURGESS, R.G. (ed.) *Educational Research and Evaluation*, London: Falmer Press.

NIAS, J., SOUTHWORTH, G. and YEOMANS, A. (1989) *Staff Relationships in the Primary School*, London: Cassells.

NIAS, J., SOUTHWORTH, G. and CAMPBELL, P. (1992) *Whole School Curriculum Development in the Primary School*. Lewes: Falmer Press.

O'CONNER, M. (1997) 'An inspector calls but then what?', *The Observer*, 19 June, p. 3.

OFSTED (1993) *The Handbook for the Inspection of Schools*, London: HMSO.

OFSTED (1995) *Corporate Plan 1995: 1995–6 to 1997–8*, London: HMSO.

OFSTIN (1997) *A Better System of Inspection*, 9 Quatre Bras, Hexham, Northumberland.

OSBORN, M. and BROADFOOT, P. (1992) 'Becoming and being a teacher: The influence of the national context', Paper presented at the British Education Research Association Conference, Stirling, September.

OUSTON, J., EARLEY, P. and FIDLER, B. (1996) (eds) *Ofsted Inspections: The Early Experience*, London: David Fulton.

PENNEY, D. and EVANS, J. (1991) 'From policy to provision: The development and "implementation" of the National Curriculum for physical education', Paper presented at St Hilda's conference, Warwick, September.

POLLARD, A., BROADFOOT, P., CROLL, P., OSBORN, M. and ABBOTT, D. (1994) *Changing English Primary Schools?: The Impact of the Education Reform Act at Key Stage One*, London: Cassell.

Power, M. (1994) *The Audit Explosion*, London: Demos.

Rafferty, F. and Dean, C. (1996) '£10,000 for a good report', *The Guardian*, 13 September, p. 5.

Rose, J. (1990) *Living the Ethnographic Life*, London: Sage.

Sandbrook, J. (1996) *Making Sense of Primary Inspection*, Buckingham: Open University Press.

Sikes, P., Measor, L. and Woods, P. (1985) *Teacher Careers: Crises and Continuities* Lewes: Falmer Press.

Smith, M.L. (1991) 'Put to the test: The effects of external testing on teachers', *Educational Researcher*, **20**, 5, pp. 8–11.

Snow, D.A. and Anderson, L. (1987) 'Identity work among the homeless: The verbal construction and avowal of personal identities', *American Journal of Sociology*, **92**, 6, pp. 1336–71.

Sugrue, C. (1997) *Complexities of Teaching: Child-centred Perspectives*, London: Falmer Press.

Thomas, W.I. (1928) *The Child in America*, New York: Knopf.

Travers, C.J. and Cooper, C.L. (1996) *Teachers under Pressure: Stress in the Teaching Profession*, London: Routledge.

Troman, G. (1996) 'Models of the good teacher', in Woods, P. (ed.) *Contemporary Issues in Teaching and Learning*, London: Routledge.

Troman, G. (1997a) 'Self-management and school inspection: Complementary forms of surveillance and control in the primary school', *Oxford Review of Education*, **23**, 3, pp. 345–64.

Troman, G. (1997b) *The effects of restructuring on primary teachers' work: a sociological analysis*, Ph.D Thesis submitted to the Open University.

Turner, V.W. (1974) *The Ritual Process*, London: Routledge and Kegan Paul.

Vulliamy, G. and Webb, R. (1993) 'Progressive education and the National Curriculum: Findings from a global education research project', *Educational Review*, **45**, 1, pp. 21–41.

Wallace, M. (1993) 'Discourse of derision: The role of the mass media within the education policy process', *Journal of Education Policy*, **8**, 4, pp. 321–37.

Webb, R. and Vulliamy, G. (1996) *Roles and Responsibilities in the Primary School*, Buckingham: Open University Press.

Wilcox, B. and Gray, J. (1996) *Inspecting Schools: Holding Schools to Account and Helping Schools to Improve*, Buckingham: Open University Press.

Woodhead, C. (1997) 'Address given to NUT/TES Conference on Progress in Partnership', *The Teacher*, November, p. 10.

Woods, P. (1979) *The Divided School*, London: Routledge and Kegan Paul.

Woods, P. (1990) *Teacher Skills and Strategies*, Lewes: Falmer Press.

Woods, P. (1993) *Critical Events in Teaching and Learning*, London: Falmer Press.

Woods, P. (1995) *Creative Teachers in Primary Schools*, Buckingham: Open University Press.

Woods, P. (1996) *Researching the Art of Teaching*, London: Routledge.

Woods, P. and Jeffrey, B. (1996a) 'A new professional discourse?: Adjusting to managerialism', in Woods, P. (ed.) *Contemporary Issues in Teaching and Learning*, London: Routledge, pp. 38–57.

Woods, P. and Jeffrey, B. (1996b) *Teachable Moments: The Art of Creative Teaching in Primary Schools*, Buckingham: Open University Press.

References

Woods, P., Jeffrey, B., Troman, G. and Boyle, M. (1997) *Restructuring Schools, Reconstructing Teachers: Responding to Change in the Primary School*, Buckingham: Open University Press.

Woods, P. and Wenham, P. (1994) 'Teaching, and researching the teaching of, a history topic: An experiment in collaboration', *The Curriculum Journal*, **5**, 2, pp. 133–61.

Woods, P. and Wenham, P. (1995) 'Politics and Pedagogy: a case study in appropriation', *Journal of Educational Policy*, **10**, 2, pp. 119–43.

Wragg, E.C. and Brighouse, T. (1995) *A New Model of School Inspection*, Exeter University School of Education: Media and Resources Centre.

Author Index

Subject Index